Battlefield Victory

Winning the War Against Satan

Battlefield Victory

Winning the War Against Satan

By Debbie Viguié

Published by Big Pink Bow

Battlefield Victory: Winning the War Against Satan

Copyright © 2013 by Debbie Viguié

ISBN-13: 978-0615938592

Published by Big Pink Bow

www.bigpinkbow.com

All rights reserved.

Verses cited in this book come from either the King James (KJV) or New King James (NKJV) versions of the Bible.

Cover art contains a photographic reproduction of *Archangel Michael* by Guido Reni

No part of this publication may be reproduced, stored in or introduced into a retrieval system, or transmitted, in any form, or by any means (electronic, mechanical, photocopying, recording, or otherwise), without prior written permission of both the copyright owner and the publisher of this book.

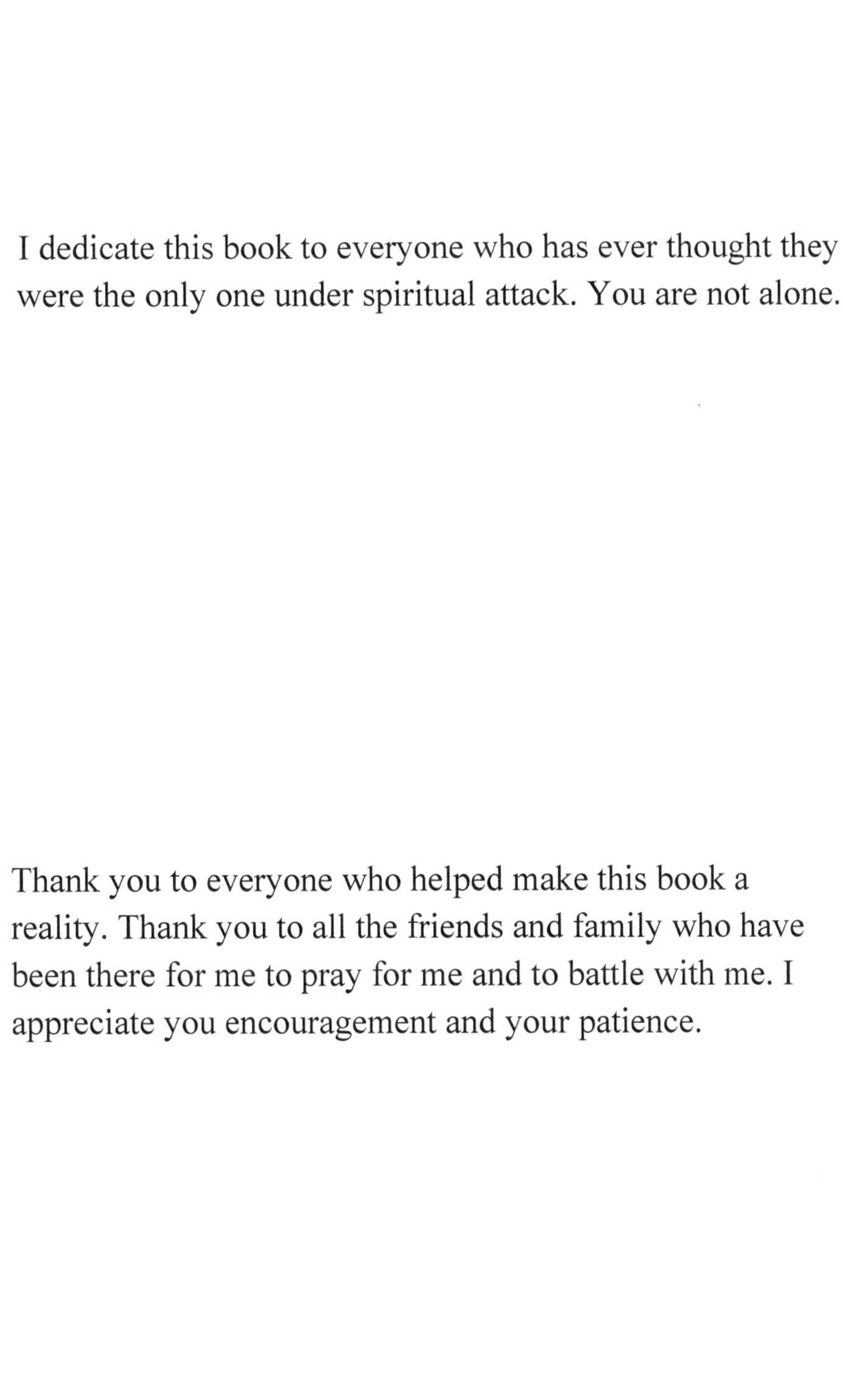

I dedicate this book to everyone who has ever thought they were the only one under spiritual attack. You are not alone.

Thank you to everyone who helped make this book a reality. Thank you to all the friends and family who have been there for me to pray for me and to battle with me. I appreciate you encouragement and your patience.

TABLE OF CONTENTS

Author's Note

I am well known for my fiction, most of which has a supernatural edge to it and depicts the battle between good and evil. What most of my readers don't know is that I have been engaged in a real-life battle with evil since I was a child. Spiritual warfare was always a very real part of my life. It wasn't always easy to talk about, though, even with those in my church or the Christian school that I attended.

As I became more experienced at fighting demons, God brought more and more people into my life who needed help with that very thing. Then God let me know that He wanted me to share my knowledge with the world. I tried to ignore that call, but God is persistent. So, here we are.

If you've picked up this book odds are good you have some inkling that evil is real and that there is an intelligence behind it. You or someone you know might have had a brush with what can only be described as evil and you're wanting to know more. You've come to the right place.

If, on the other hand, you've just picked this up out of curiosity, rest assured, there is still a lot in here you can learn and benefit from. That's because we are all plagued by demons in one form or another, even when we're not aware of it. These range from real, living entities with minds of their own to unthinking impulses and torments of our own creation.

The goal of this book is to educate and enlighten. It's my desire to help every person in the world learn to vanquish the demons that torment them or hold them hostage. This book is written primarily for the Protestant Christian, however, others may learn from it as well.

One more thing. DON'T DESPAIR. You've come to the right place for answers and help. God grant you a clear mind as you read through this book and bind any demons through the power of Christ's blood shed on the cross for our sins so that they may not stop you from reading, understanding, and acting upon the message you are about to receive.

Chapter 1
Yes, Virginia, There is a Satan

First and foremost, I want to be very clear on one thing. There is a Satan. Different cultures have different names for him, but there is one fallen angel who serves as the ultimate, malevolent intelligence in the universe and coordinates the efforts of all other evil spirits. He is in no way, shape or form equal to God. Like angels, humans, and animals he is a created being. That means he is fallible and in no way omnipotent despite what he wants people to think. God is in charge and Satan's power is only equivalent to that of other angels. He just uses his for evil in an effort to cause mankind to fall away from God and heed their own baser urges instead of striving to be their best and highest selves as God intended.

His motives have been long speculated on. Some believe that jealousy of humans caused his fall. Others have speculated that an arrogant belief that he was equal to God led to the revolution in heaven that saw him and his followers cast out. The Jewish people believe he isn't evil at all, but that he is an angel of God doing the task God has set for him which is to oppose people and help them to grow stronger because of it. Some religions see him as one of a pantheon of gods, but the one dedicated to chaos, mischief, and harm.

Ultimately whatever his motives are doesn't matter. Whatever religious background you come from and whether you view him as an angel, a fallen angel, or a dark god doesn't affect the basic fact that he is to be resisted and defeated both in your life and in the cosmic scheme of things. For the purposes of this book we will speak of him with the Christian perspective of the chief of the fallen angels, enemy of both God and man.

I have had the great dishonor of encountering him face-to-face on roughly half a dozen occasions. The first was as a young child when he revealed himself to me for the purpose of terrorizing me and dissuading me from the plan God had for my life. Many years later when I had answered God's call to be a warrior for Him and help teach others about spiritual warfare Satan again came to me and offered me a deal in order to stop me from speaking of what I knew to others and battling him openly. I refused and the last few encounters with him have been as equally unpleasant as those.

The vast majority of people will never encounter Satan themselves. His appearances to people are thankfully infrequent. He doesn't have to show up because there are legions who do his bidding and the torment and confusion they bring is more than enough to trap people in a perpetual darkness of despair, pain, and ineffectualness. Even the least demon can cause unspeakable havoc in a person's life.

This is why any demonic attack, no matter how slight or from where it comes should be treated with the utmost seriousness and quick and decisive action. We will get into how to recognize and deal with attacks in later chapters.

SATAN AND THE BIBLE

Satan is mentioned by name more than fifty times in the Bible. Devils, demons, or unclean spirits are mentioned more than seventy times. Job was tormented by Satan himself who had to receive permission from God to do so. Jesus was tempted by Satan. Jesus and his followers cast out demons and unclean spirits as part of their ministry. The war between God and Satan comes to a climax in the book of Revelation where we are given a taste of the things to come.

In the Bible these evil creatures are given just as much weight and credence as angels. Both exist. There have been many modern movements that want to deny the existence of the evil spirits while still acknowledging the good ones. This is simply not Biblical. It is not even logical. God's creation shows a balance and harmony between all things including light and dark, male and female. To put it in scientific terms for every action there is an equal and opposite reaction. Evil does not just sit in the human heart. It also has a consciousness and a form and can express itself when and where it chooses.

This movement to deny the existence of evil made it hard for many years to talk about the reality of it. When I first began to open up and share my own experiences it was with a great deal of trepidation because I knew that there was a decent chance that the person I was talking to, even if a professed Christian, would not believe me.

I've been very surprised and relieved that it has become easier in recent years to discuss this subject freely and openly. We must bring these things out of the darkness and into the light so that we can best understand how to help ourselves and each other.

Here are just a few of the things the Bible has to say about Satan that are true and relevant and important for people to remember:

- "Be sober, be vigilant; because your adversary the devil walks about like a roaring lion, seeking whom he may devour." - I Peter 5:8 (NKJV)

- "Submit yourselves therefore to God. Resist the devil, and he will flee from you." - James 4:7 (KJV)

- "And these are they by the way side, where the word is sown; but when they have heard, Satan cometh immediately, and taketh away the word that was sown in their hearts." - Mark 4:15 (KJV)

- "And he said to them, 'I saw Satan fall like lightning from heaven'." - Luke 10:18 (NKJV)

- "And the God of peace shall bruise Satan under your feet shortly. The grace of our Lord Jesus Christ be with you. Amen." - Romans 16:20 (KJV)

SATAN IN THE MODERN WORLD

The activities of Satan and his minions didn't cease after the early church. Satan and the demons under him have been busy the last two millennia making life difficult for everyone. His goal is to keep believers from reaching their God-given potential and to keep non-believers from becoming believers. To that end he tempts us and torments us.

The devil doesn't tempt us when we are at our best. When we are strong, confident, secure, and want for nothing it is harder to shake us. This was the very argument he gave God concerning Job in fact. So, you'll notice that it was after Jesus had been fasting for forty days and was hungry (and isolated and likely very weak physically) that Satan put in his appearance. And he didn't just tempt Jesus in one area, he tempted him in several. These same categories are areas in which he tempts us.

Physical Needs - The desire to fulfill physical needs (food, shelter, etc.) are the most basic needs a human being has. They can be the easiest to fulfill, but when life goes wrong they can sometimes seem impossible to achieve. Here it was food. Jesus had to be incredibly hungry. So, Satan tempts him with turning stones to bread. On the surface, this doesn't even seem like a terrible idea. I mean, he didn't ask him to steal or cheat or lie, just use his gifts to feed himself. In the same way, Satan will tempt us in subtle ways, often with things that aren't even illegal or immoral, just questionable. Where's the harm? he asks. Fasting was a religious exercise for the Jews, a way of purifying the body and allowing the mind to focus more fully on God. Satan often wants to take our minds off God and put them on ourselves.

Emotional or Ego Needs - Power and glory. Very few people if they are being honest with themselves don't want these things. Yet, look at what Satan was offering Jesus. It's ludicrous for two reasons. First, Jesus' whole message was about the kingdom of God, the kingdom that was to come. What Satan was talking about was the idea of the earthly kingdom that the Jews were expecting their Messiah to lead. Playing into human expectations. Second, it's ludicrous because God owns everything already. He is only allowing Satan to play in His sandbox. So, Satan was offering Jesus what was not his offer. It's like if someone walked up to your car and offered to give it to you if you would just worship them. It's already your car. No brainer. So, why this temptation? Because it would have been attractive to Jesus to unite the world in peace under Him now, but that was not the plan. The glory and power that He ultimately would have far transcended that of what Satan was offering. He just had to stick to the plan and remember that shortcuts are often pitfalls in disguise.

WHAT DOES WARFARE LOOK LIKE?

Warfare can take many forms, most of them subtle. A string of strange coincidences that keep you from achieving something that would benefit you, others, or the kingdom of God could be an attack. Persistent negative thoughts and emotions that distract you and keep you from being productive could be an attack.

Attacks can also be far more obvious and include seeing or hearing things when you are alone. They can turn violent in the most extreme cases.

The bottom line is, anything that is keeping you from achieving your potential and doing the work of God is potentially an attack by the enemy that must be responded to. In Chapter 2 we will discuss basic strategies for beginning to fight back and in Chapter 3 we will discuss how to determine if what is happening to you is a spiritual attack. IF you are experiencing physical attacks go now immediately to Chapter 2 for help.

WHAT DEMONS CAN'T DO

Demons can manipulate you, harass you, and even harm you physically at times. As a Protestant, however, they can NOT possess you in the traditional sense of the word. They can't step into your body and take over. They can possess others, but not you. Instead they are oppressing you.

WHY YOU?

A lot of times when we go through something horrific, we find ourselves asking "Why?" If things are really bad we might even find ourselves screaming "Why?" and begging God for an answer. When it comes to spiritual warfare, this is a simple question to answer.

Satan and all the demons under his control hate you and want you to fail and turn away from God. That's right. They hate you. That's the first reason you are suffering. They want you to fail. They don't want you to be the person you could be, to succeed and fulfill your potential. That's the second reason. They want you to turn away from God. That's the third reason. Satan was convinced if he could torment Job enough that Job would turn from God. It didn't work with Job, but it has worked on others.

You are unique and special. That's how God created you. You were made in His image and the life that He has set out for you is a life and path that no one else can live and take. They're all for you. God has an ideal plan in mind for you. Many things can keep us from sticking to this plan, most notably our own stubbornness, fear, or short-sightedness. However, Satan and his minions can also attack you to try and get you to stray from the path and veer from the plan. But why you ask?

It doesn't matter if you're a minister or a missionary, your life, your example, is seen by thousands and thousands of people in your lifetime. Without saying a word about what you believe, you are demonstrating it in your actions, your words, even the way you carry yourself when you walk down the street. There is something about a Christian living out their potential that acts like a beacon to bring others to God, even if they never mention His name to those people.

To stop us from doing this, demons hit us where it hurts, where they think they can do the most damage. They know our Achilles heels and they continue to thrash away on them hoping to destroy us. They have studied us and know how best to stop us from reaching our God-given potential and being the people, the Christians, that God has called us to be.

When we are at our best, fulfilling God's dream for our life, we are reaching more people through our example. Often we are touching lives more directly as well. God might be calling you to create a business, start a ministry, get involved with a charity, or otherwise help people in a real, measurable way. Satan wants to stop this at all costs.

So, Satan sends his minions to attack you.

That's what they're doing now. Here's a couple of questions to ponder while you continue reading.

What was happening in your spiritual life before the attack? (Think about the hours before, but also the days and weeks.)

What do you think the Enemy might be trying to distract you from or stop you from doing?

These questions will help you understand why and when attacks happen. Still, it can be hard to determine sometimes when you are under attack or when the things that are happening to you are simply part of the natural world and not the supernatural. Determining the difference is what we discuss in Chapter 3.

KEY SCRIPTURES

"Be sober, be vigilant; because your adversary the devil walks about like a roaring lion, seeking whom he may devour."

- I Peter 5:8 (NKJV)

"Submit yourselves therefore to God. Resist the devil, and he will flee from you."

- James 4:7 (KJV)

"And these are they by the way side, where the word is sown; but when they have heard, Satan cometh immediately, and taketh away the word that was sown in their hearts."

- Mark 4:15 (KJV)

"And he said to them, 'I saw Satan fall like lightning from heaven'."

- Luke 10:18 (NKJV)

"And the God of peace shall bruise Satan under your feet shortly. The grace of our Lord Jesus Christ be with you. Amen."

- Romans 16:20 (KJV)

ACTION STEPS

- Take a deep breath and admit that Satan wants to stop you from fulfilling God's plan for your life.
- Ask yourself if there has been anything unusual going on in your life in any aspect that seems negative or is hindering you.
- Ask yourself what was happening in your spiritual life at the time the unusual thing began to happen.
- Ask yourself what it is that God might want you to do that Satan would not want you to do.

PRAYER OF VICTORY

Thank You, God, for opening my eyes to the reality of the spiritual war that is raging around me. Help me as I learn to defend myself and drive the enemy from my life. Thank You that I already have the victory through You. Amen.

Chapter 2
The Most Basic Principles of War

There are two crucial things that everyone facing spiritual warfare must know **and** remember in order to survive with body, mind, and spirit intact. First, demons can't do anything to us without God's permission and God will never allow us to be tested beyond what we are capable of bearing. Second, you have the power to banish demons from your life. Remember these two things and you are well on your way to victory.

SPIRITUAL WARFARE, THE BIBLE, AND YOU

When Satan tormented Job, he had to first get permission from God to do so. Satan told God that the only reason Job was righteous was because God showed him favor.

> "And the LORD said to Satan, 'Behold, all that he has *is* in your power; only do not lay a hand on his *person.*' So Satan went out from the presence of the LORD." - Job 1:12 (NKJV)

Later, frustrated by the fact that he hadn't gotten Job to turn against God, Satan had to petition to be allowed to attack him with physical illness. God allowed Satan to do so, but told him he couldn't kill Job. This exchange takes place in Job 2:1-6.

Now, in case you're tempted to think that Job was a special case, and that demons don't need permission from God to harm you, consider these verses:

> "Ye are of God, little children, and have overcome them: because greater is he that is in you, than he that is in the world." - I John 4:4 (KJV)

> "There hath no temptation taken you but such as is common to man: but God is faithful, who will not suffer you to be tempted above that ye are able; but will with the temptation also make a way to escape, that ye may be able to bear it." - I Chronicles 10:13 (NKJV)

This was not an isolated event. Jesus himself was tempted by Satan. Jesus withstood the temptations and triumphed over the attacks, thus allowing all of us a chance at salvation and reconciliation with God. Just as he defeated Satan, so can we. God has all power and we, as His heirs, should take comfort that our Father is in control and is looking out for us. Why then let us encounter such monsters at all you might ask? For the same reason that any human parent allows their child to go out into the dangerous world. To teach us, to help us grow, and to help us become the men and women He has shown us how to be that our light might shine forth and reach those who have not come to Him. The apostle said it best:

> "My brethren, count it all joy when ye fall into divers temptations; Knowing this, that the trying of your faith worketh patience. But let patience have her perfect

work, that ye may be perfect and entire, wanting nothing." - James 1:2-4 (KJV)

Now, only a saint could see joy in these situations, but hopefully we can all see the reason. It's easier to endure hardship when you understand why it is happening and what the outcome will be.

The short term outcome of us surviving and overcoming demonic attack? The betterment of ourselves as people, as Christians. The long term outcome of spiritual warfare? God is going to kick Satan's tail into hell for the rest of time and we'll be free of him. Now that's a victory worth celebrating! In fact, it's a victory worth celebrating now, because we know it is absolutely going to happen. Satan has already lost, he just hasn't been locked up yet. There's a popular saying, "The next time the devil reminds you of your past, remind him of his future." I like that. It's a tool to remind you of what's important, what the big picture is, and to keep you from letting Satan use your past and your feelings about it to manipulate you in the present and ruin your future.

Many of you have heard of the faith of the mustard seed. Scripture tells us:

> "And Jesus said unto them, 'Because of your unbelief: for verily I say unto you, If ye have faith as a grain of mustard seed, ye shall say unto this mountain, Remove hence to yonder place; and it shall remove; and nothing shall be impossible unto you.'" - Matthew 17:20 (KJV)

This verse is one of the most powerful, and the most challenging, in the New Testament. However, many people forget the context. What exactly was it the disciples hadn't been able to do that Jesus told them was because of their unbelief? They had been unable to cast a demon out of a young man. Read here the entire passage:

> "And when they were come to the multitude, there came to him a certain man, kneeling down to him, and saying, Lord, have mercy on my son: for he is lunatick, and sore vexed: for ofttimes he falleth into the fire, and oft into the water. And I brought him to thy disciples, and they could not cure him. Then Jesus answered and said, O faithless and perverse generation, how long shall I be with you? how long shall I suffer you? bring him hither to me. And Jesus rebuked the devil; and he departed out of him: and the child was cured from that very hour. Then came the disciples to Jesus apart, and said, Why could not we cast him out? And Jesus said unto them, Because of your unbelief: for verily I say unto you, If ye have faith as a grain of mustard seed, ye shall say unto this mountain, Remove hence to yonder place; and it shall remove; and nothing shall be impossible unto you. Howbeit this kind goeth not out but by prayer and fasting." - Matthew 17:14-21 (KJV)

So, remember, God is bigger than Satan, Jesus has already defeated Satan, and everything Satan does to you is aimed at getting you to forget the truth of that. He wants you to live a small life of fear and isolation without ever reaching your true potential. Satan wants to take as many people with him as he can. So why torment those who already believe? Simple. To steal your power and to keep you from being a light in the darkness that others can see. He doesn't want you to influence anyone in any way to turn to God. And when he gets us so wrapped up in our own heads he does just that. He is a creature obsessed with bondage and slavery and he wants to see the entire human race that way.

Which is exactly why we have to stand up and push back and claim the freedom that Christ paid for with his blood. We have to do it, not just for ourselves and our family, but for all those lost souls out there waiting for someone to show them the way.

COMMANDING DEMONS TO LEAVE

Demons often appear to know us quite well. There is good reason for this, but it should not be a cause for extra fear. That is playing into their hands. Every time they get you to react out of fear they win. Ignoring them isn't the answer either. You can ignore the snake in the grass, but it can still bite you. No, demons must be faced and dealt with firmly, with full faith in the power of God and the authority He gave us over them.

That's right. We have power over them. Satan's entire strategy is based on fear and intimidation and keeping us from ever realizing or acting on the fact that we are the ones with all the power, we hold the cards, and we say whether they stay or go.

But how on earth can we possibly affect them you might ask? The answer is simple. COMMAND THEM TO LEAVE.

Take a moment and reflect on those four words. Notice I said "command" and not "ask". We do not need their permission to get rid of them. We do not need God to intervene on our behalf to get it done. We need to take responsibility and order them to get away from us.

And guess what? If we do it with conviction and faith, they have to obey. How awesome is that?

Here's what I say:

In the name of Jesus Christ whose blood was shed on the cross for the forgiveness of my sins, I rebuke you, I bind you, and I command you to leave, right NOW!

If at all possible say this out loud, shout it if you can, but whisper it if you have to. It's easier to put your faith and passion into the words if you speak them than if you think them and they will be more effective. If you have to think them, focus as hard as you can and feel the faith and passion in you as you think them clearly and distinctly. Again, it's easier to speak if you can, but don't despair if you can't.

You can use my command, or work up one of your own. It is important to invoke the blood of Christ. After all, that's what restored our connection to God and defeated Satan. It's the source of our power and his defeat.

You can also address God, Jesus, or the Holy Spirit inside you to help you with the task, but remember, <u>you must take personal responsibility for making the demons leave</u>. Jesus did this and taught the disciples as well. So, next time a demon is harassing you, command them to leave. Go ahead, try it.

WHAT'S NEXT?

You've done it! You've gotten a demon or multiple demons to leave the building. Literally. Now what? Here's one of the crucial parts. They can come back and so you might need to command them to leave several times. Do not let your conviction waver! Command them each time like it's going to be the one and only time you have to do so. Do not give them even an inch to try and come back faster or stronger or even at all. You must do what you can as well to shore up the weak parts of your life that they keep attacking. As long as it bothers you, they will be attracted to it as a means of stopping you.

Also, it's a good idea at this point to do a thorough cleansing and blessing of your home, your office, even your car. Any place that you spend a lot of time is a potential hotbed of demonic activity. How do you go about blessing a space? It's actually fairly simple. In your home, enter each room, place a hand on one of the walls, and claim the space for God. Command all demonic entities and negative energy to leave and never return. If it helps, visualize a bright, white light cleansing and scouring the room. Go from room to room doing this. In your office, put your hand on the wall of the room, the wall of your cubicle, your desk, your equipment, whatever really encompasses your work space and do the same thing. As with commanding demons to leave it's always best to say the words out loud if you can. Do the same for your car.

If you wish you can buy a small bottle of oil that some religious stores sell for purposes of anointing and healing. If this helps you visualize and helps you feel the faith and strength and conviction of what you're doing, go for it. Otherwise, it is not necessary.

For particularly intense or sustained periods of demonic attack, be prepared to do this more than once. If things are particularly bad for you and demons are hounding you at every turn, do this at least once a week until things improve.

Now work on claiming victory for God in those areas of your life that you are being harassed in. This can include health, relationships, finances, areas of sin and addiction. Now's the time to give these things over to God and work to make everything right insofar as you can. There are some good books out there that can help you in these areas.

KEY SCRIPTURES

"And when they were come to the multitude, there came to him a certain man, kneeling down to him, and saying, Lord, have mercy on my son: for he is lunatick, and sore vexed: for ofttimes he falleth into the fire, and oft into the water. And I brought him to thy disciples, and they could not cure him. Then Jesus answered and said, O faithless and perverse generation, how long shall I be with you? how long shall I suffer you? bring him hither to me. And Jesus rebuked the devil; and he departed out of him: and the child was cured from that very hour. Then came the disciples to Jesus apart, and said, Why could not we cast him out? And Jesus said unto them, Because of your unbelief: for verily I say unto you, If ye have faith as a grain of mustard seed, ye shall say unto this mountain, Remove hence to yonder place; and it shall remove; and nothing shall be impossible unto you. Howbeit this kind goeth not out but by prayer and fasting."

- Matthew 17:14-21 (KJV)

"And Jesus rebuked him, saying, Hold thy peace, and come out of him. And when the devil had thrown him in the midst, he came out of him, and hurt him not."

- Luke 4:35 (KJV)

"'And these signs will follow those who believe: In My name they will cast out demons; they will speak with new tongues;'"

- Mark 16:17 (NKJV)

ACTION STEPS

- Out loud, right now, command any demons who are harassing you in any way to get out in the name of Jesus Christ whose blood was shed on the cross for the forgiveness of your sins. Shout it if you can.
- Bless and pray for your home and any other places where you have experienced an attack.

PRAYER OF VICTORY

Thank You, God, that I don't have to live in fear and confusion but that I can live a strong, victorious life in

You. Thank You for giving me authority to drive out demons and help me to know when it is time to do so. Protect me and guide me as I fight. Amen.

Chapter 3
How to Recognize When the Monsters in The Closet Are Real

You swear you see something moving in the closet when you've left the door open. You have an unreasoning fear that something is lurking under the bed waiting to grab your ankle. You are convinced that if you look into the bathroom mirror in the dead of night something else will be staring back at you.

Do any of these sound familiar? They should. These are fairly common childhood fears which have been played upon and exploited in popular culture and myth. Probably ninety percent of the time they are just that, fears. It's the other ten percent that you have to be concerned about.

I don't envy my parents. I was targeted by demons starting at a young age and I know it could not have been easy on them. By day I was a very happy, smart, logical child. By night I insisted on a closed closet door, wouldn't dangle any body parts over the edge of my bed, and kept my eyes shut the entire time if I had to get up in the middle of the night to go to the bathroom because I was terrified of what I might see.

Of course, I was also an avid reader and a budding writer with a very vivid imagination which made me my own worst enemy. That didn't mean that the monsters weren't all too often real. Although I was targeted and plagued by these entities I'm happy to report that nothing ever grabbed me from under the bed until after I was an adult.

When it comes to determining whether or not there is a demon present or you're merely jumping at shadows or having a terrible day you have to be alert. Also, if you are a parent, you have an extra responsibility. Listen to your children when they tell you that something is frightening them. Kids often pick up on a lot more than adults do in the spiritual area because they haven't learned how to ignore it yet or convince themselves that it's their imagination. You have to be very careful not to instill further fear in your child or add fuel to the fire of their imaginations, but you must at least consider whether their concerns are truly valid. This can be a difficult line to walk that will require you to be very calm and exude a sense of understanding and authority.

The basic question that you need to answer before you can do anything about a demonic attack is this: How do you know if something is just your imagination or you really are being targeted by a demon?

Before you can properly defend yourself against an attack you have to realize that you are under attack. Please note, that if you have any question in your mind whatsoever about this that you should go ahead and act as if you are to be on the safe side. Command the demons to leave and take steps to cleanse the environment if you have to.

For those who want or need a little more clarification and help identifying attacks here are some very simple guidelines which are by no means all-inclusive. There are two types of attacks: direct and indirect.

HOW TO TELL IF YOU ARE UNDER DIRECT DEMONIC ATTACK

Of the two types of demonic attack, direct attacks are the most obvious and much, much rarer. Most people will never experience a direct attack, but here are some indicators that you might be.

- You may SEE movement out of the corner of your eyes, black shadows in the room that move around or seem out of place or darker than they should be, strange things reflected in the mirror.

- You may HEAR frightening sounds, voices taunting you, and scratching noises. These may be inside or outside your head.

- You may SMELL something sulfurous or otherwise foul.

- You may FEEL your heart pounding, dizziness/light-headedness, chills racing up your spine, hair standing up on the back of your neck, a presence in the room with you, something grab you, touch you, or in very, very rare cases, attempt to strangle you.

- PAY ATTENTION to your animals. If your normally calm dog becomes agitated and starts barking at a particular spot or refuses to go into a certain room, that could be a sign that he is seeing what you're not.

The most important thing you can do at this point is to remain calm and remember the two basic facts about demons. They cannot do anything to you without God's permission **AND** you have the power to banish them. So, take a deep breath and tell them to get away from you and out of the building.

Once they are gone, pray that God sets up a barrier around the place that you are in so that those or other demons may not enter. Please note, this barrier will only be a temporary one and so asking God to do this once does not protect the room indefinitely. This will give you time to stop and breathe, though, and figure out if there's anything you need to do. If you have had this type of experience you are almost certainly going to want to cleanse the space you're in to rid it of any leftover demonic residue. Picture it as black slime that they can leave behind when they go and bless and consecrate the room to God and ask for His help purging and cleansing it. A simple way to do this is place your hand on a wall of the room and pray over the room, giving it to God. In extreme cases, do it for every wall in the room. If it helps you, you may add anointing or blessing oil that you can pick up at a Christian bookstore.

HOW TO TELL IF YOU ARE UNDER INDIRECT DEMONIC ATTACK

Direct attacks make up a very tiny portion of all demonic attacks. Most demonic attacks are far more subtle and indirect. This can also make them harder to detect and can allow them to go on for extended periods of time without you being aware of what is happening. Some signs of indirect attack include:

- Unnatural, overly intense negative emotions particularly for extended periods of time or out of context to what is happening in your life

- Violent and destructive thoughts, particularly ones that aren't common to you or seem unusually intense or out-of-control

- Sudden impulses to do harm to yourself or others

- Being trapped in destructive behaviors and feeling that you don't have the power to make a change

- Loss of interest or inability to pray, read the Bible, or engage in other spiritual activities. Please note, these should mark a change in attitude or behavior. If you've been meaning to get around to reading your Bible or attend church regularly for years that is likely a whole different problem. This is a change in your normal activity often accompanied by feelings of lethargy, uselessness, dread, or sudden disinterest

- Crippling depression and anxiety with no easily treatable or fixable medical or environmental cause

- Endless distractions that keep you from fulfilling promises you make to yourself and God about the things you are going to do particularly in relation to your spiritual walk, your ministry, or your connections to other people

- Isolating and cutting yourself off from people who can help you
- Persistent and undiagnosed health problems that are distracting or debilitating
- Unexplained agitation from a family pet or young child usually linked to one area of the house which can last for minutes or days
- Avoidance of particular areas of the house, often at nighttime (this can sometimes be your mind trying to tell you something)
- Exhaustion disproportionate to what you should be feeling
- Crippling fear and feelings of dread that keep you from doing things you want or need to do
- A sensation of being ill-at-ease
- Awareness that certain thoughts you have or actions you do seem out of character and somehow foreign to you
- Being told by friends or family that there's something different, usually darker, about you

This list is by no means comprehensive and it does require some discernment as many of the items on there can also be attributed to illness, medications, elevated amounts of stress, or problems at home or at work. You must carefully consider what is natural and unnatural given your own circumstances and your own psyche. A human being on their best days can be lazy, stubborn, and slow to change. This is where the better you know yourself, the better off you'll be. You'll learn to spot demonic attacks more quickly and end them in minutes instead of months.

HOW TO TELL IF FRIENDS OR FAMILY ARE UNDER DEMONIC ATTACK

Sometimes you are not the one under attack but a friend or family member is. The signs are generally the same in others as those you would look for in yourself. Be concerned if the other person begins to display any of the following signs.

- Sudden loss of interest in spiritual matters
- Personality changes for the negative
- Sudden interest in movies, books, or music of a dark or depressing nature
- Attempts at self-injury or suicide
- Sudden lack of care for their physical appearance

- Panic attacks, sustained depression, despair
- Violent mood swings, unpredictable behavior, paranoia
- Inability to cope with day-to-day life
- Engaging in behaviors or sins that would normally be abhorrent to them
- Reckless disregard for their own safety
- Isolating from those who love them and could help them

Again, there can be natural underlying causes for many of the things on this list. Make sure you rule out natural possibilities for these symptoms.

BEING AWARE OF THE TIMING OF DEMONIC ATTACKS

Another tool you can use when determining if you are under a spiritual attack is to look at your current circumstances. It is the goal of demons to keep you from living your God-given destiny, fulfilling your potential, and having the most excellent life you possibly can. If you are just coasting along life's highway doing nothing to stretch, grow, fulfill your own destiny or challenge Satan's hold on this earth or its inhabitants, odds are good you are going to experience very few demonic attacks. If you are doing nothing to actively improve your own life, further your relationship with God, expand His kingdom, or free others from the tyranny of evil, then Satan's got you where he wants you. Why rock the boat?

There are, obviously, exceptions to this which are often based on our potential and the possibilities of what we might do with it either in the near or distant future. Satan and his minions worked very hard for a great number of years to keep me so terrified and off-balance that I couldn't strike back and bring God's message of freedom from demonic oppression to people. In that case it wasn't anything I was actively doing, but something the forces of evil wanted to stop me from ever doing.

If nothing in your life has changed and you are experiencing sudden demonic attack, know that God has a plan for you coming up, a life you're supposed to touch, a new direction you're supposed to take, or a growth spurt that Satan wants to make sure you are too distracted to even notice.

Most of the time, though, Satan attacks when you are actively trying to deepen your relationship with God, help other people, or fulfill your potential as a person and as a Christian. In that regard, you can actually begin to use demonic attack as a sign that you are on the right path and doing what you are supposed to be doing.

So, when you're trying to decide if you're being attacked by a demon or if the things that are happening to you have natural causes or are springing from your imagination, look at what is happening in your life. Ask yourself these questions:

- Am I challenging and stretching myself as a person or as a Christian?
- Have I begun a new career, business, or ministry?
- Am I trying to be part of a new relationship of some sort?
- Have I been talking to a non-Christian about God?
- Have others been asking me about my spiritual walk or asking me for advice?
- Am I trying to understand God's destiny for me?
- Am I trying to reconcile myself to my past or to a person?
- Is there something new and positive in my life?
- Am I thinking about or planning to make a new, positive change soon?

If you answered yes to any of these questions, the odds that what you are experiencing is actually demonic have gone up. Of particular importance is your impact on other people. If you are talking to others about a relationship with God, you can bet the enemy is furious about that. If you have even the slightest chance of reaching that person, odds are the enemy is furious enough to do something about it.

One of the single most intense periods of spiritual warfare in my entire life came in college when my roommate was grappling with becoming a Christian. I was grabbed, chased, and daily tormented by demons who did not want her to have a relationship with God. They were terrified of her finding Him and fulfilling her own destiny. The daily flood of attacks went on for months, intensifying after she became a Christian. Demons actually tried to kill her and I was very clear about the fact that my job was to stop them from succeeding. They finally gave up.

Another period of intense attack came when I decided I wanted to make my living as a writer. A third period of intense attack came when I finally stopped ignoring God's call to share what I have experienced of spiritual warfare with others.

So, knowing what you know of your own life and how you are living it and the choices that you are currently making can be of real benefit when determining if there is something out there trying to stop you. Of equal importance is learning where your vulnerable spots are.

BE AWARE OF YOUR OWN ACHILLES HEEL

Demons know how to hit us where it hurts. For some they attack health, for others relationships, still other people they try to mess with their finances. What's difficult about these types of attacks is that they are all things that can go wrong completely on their own from natural causes without any supernatural interference whatsoever. That said, there are often smaller, very specific things that can really torment us individually that demons will use against us and that we can use to recognize as a sign of demonic interference.

For me, for the longest time, it was cockroaches.

We had an opportunity to achieve our dream and move to Hawaii. We found a nice condo on a lovely part of the island of Kauai. I even sold my first Christian fiction series within a few days of moving. It was like a dream come true.

And then the cockroaches turned my dream into a nightmare. They were everywhere. I even found them inside the freezer. The condo complex sprayed, but clearly not often enough, and our landlord who lived in another state didn't really care. It became a daily battle of us versus them. I'd wake up every morning to find ten or so dead or dying and another ten that I'd have to try to squish.

It didn't matter what we did, they just kept coming. I didn't even stop to think about the fact that it was a time of intense spiritual growth for me where I was actually committing to starting up a ministry to help people deal with their demonic issues.

When I finally reached the point where I was able to squash cockroaches that were several inches long without screaming each time things intensified. They started landing on our faces while we were asleep. One night I got up to use the restroom and one flew out of an overhead vent and right down into my pajama top. My screaming woke up not only my husband, but also I'm pretty sure the neighbors as well.

We finally moved and embarked on a period where life was much busier, more complicated, and my ministry had to be placed on the backburner. We made sure that we had pest control people who were out spraying routinely and we had no problems with insects of any kind. Then, one day, I had a moment of spiritual breakthrough and within an hour I found a huge cockroach sitting in the middle of our living room.

That was when I knew that in my life cockroaches are a sign of demonic interference. I squished that cockroach, told the demon who had gotten it there exactly where to go, and have learned to take the cockroaches of life in stride and to immediately look for something darker at work.

Cockroaches are a part of the natural world, but to me, they are a particular torment that they wouldn't be to most people. It's when I learned to not let myself be upset by them that demons finally stopped using them to get under my skin and distract me from whatever it is I'm trying to do. One still shows up occasionally with clearly suspicious timing. I take it as a sign that I'm on the right path.

Look for the thing that will make you hysterical, that will distract you and throw you off your game no matter what. Then, when it shows up in your life, use it as a sign that you should check to see if something bigger and nastier is trying to disrupt your day or even a particular task.

GETTING IN TOUCH WITH THE HOLY SPIRIT

The Holy Spirit indwells us as Christians. The Holy Spirit also knows the difference between a demon and a shadow. The more time you spend learning to listen to that still, small voice, being open to the promptings of the Spirit, the better off you are. This actually applies to every area of your life, but for our purposes it is especially helpful when dealing with demons.

Ask God to give you the gift of discernment so that you might know the difference between imaginings and actual attacks. The more you learn to listen, to feel, to get in tune, the easier it will become.

As a simple exercise try closing your eyes. Picture the room that you're in as though you're looking down on it like a rough drawing, like a floor plan. Ask God to show you where in the room the demons are. You may or may not see or sense a particular spot on the floor plan right away. If you don't see anything, it could mean that nothing is there or that you need to spend more time learning to understand what the Spirit has to say on this matter. You can take this same principal and apply it to an entire building such as a house.

DON'T TAKE CHANCES

If you suspect that you are under spiritual attack, act to put an end to it. It's better to act when you don't have to than to be passive when you should be doing something. If done right you can even use this technique to help make your children feel more secure. When in doubt, do something, because it can't hurt you, but doing nothing when something is there can cause no end of suffering.

It takes a long time to get truly accurate about the presence, location, number, or types of demons afflicting you. That doesn't mean it's okay to sit by and do nothing. Remember, always err on the side of caution. Eventually you will get better at identifying these things, but remember, Satan is sneaky and he isn't called the Father of Lies for nothing. Demons have perfected the art of the sneak attack.

There are times when even I need a trusted friend to point out that I'm under attack, and I've been dealing with this for decades. It's okay to ask for a second opinion from someone you trust. And it's always okay to pray and ask for God's protection and to cast out any evil spirits in His name.

KEY SCRIPTURES

"Then the seventy returned with joy, saying, 'Lord, even the demons are subject to us in Your name.' And He said to them, 'I saw Satan fall like lightning from heaven. Behold, I give you the authority to trample on serpents and scorpions, and over all the power of the enemy, and nothing shall by any means hurt you. Nevertheless do not rejoice in this, that the spirits are subject to you, but rather rejoice because your names are written in heaven.'"

- Luke 10:17-20

"And there are diversities of activities, but it is the same God who works all in all. But the manifestation of the Spirit is given to each one for the profit of all: for to one is given the word of wisdom through the Spirit, to another the word of knowledge through the same Spirit, to another faith by the same Spirit, to another gifts of healings by the same Spirit, to another the working of miracles, to another prophecy, to another discerning of spirits, to another different kinds of tongues, to another the interpretation of

tongues. But one and the same Spirit works all these things, distributing to each one individually as He wills."
- I Corinthians 12:6-11 (NKJV)

ACTION STEPS

- Ask the Holy Spirit to help you figure out when you or a loved one are under spiritual attack.
- When in doubt, banish any demons in the name of Jesus Christ whose blood was shed on the cross for the forgiveness of your sins.
- Practice imagining rooms or buildings and trying to see if there seems to be any demons present.
- Examine your life and see where you are spiritually and where it is you are going.
- Understand what your Achilles heel is and where demons are likely to attack you that will be very specific to you. Learn to see such attacks as a sign that you're doing something right and banish the demon responsible.

PRAYER OF VICTORY

Thank You, God, for opening my eyes to the ways in which demons are attacking me and those around me. Thank you that I have the victory over them because of Christ's sacrifice on the cross. Help me to continue to grow in You and help me to not be bothered when demons try and push my buttons. Amen.

Chapter 4
Personal Demons, Family Demons, and Created Demons, Oh My!

Not all demons are created equal. Not all demons are even created the same way. There are, in fact, four principal types of demons. They are: personal demons, family demons, created demons, and fallen angels. Tactics for dealing with all of these demons are basically similar, but there are special considerations to be taken into account for each type of demon. While most people will never encounter a fallen angel, everyone is plagued with at least one personal demon which they must defeat to reach their true potential.

PERSONAL DEMONS

It's not uncommon to hear the phrase "personal demon". It's used frequently to reference someone's struggles in a certain area, such as alcoholism, violence, etc. The two things most people don't realize is that the term isn't just a figure of speech and that everyone has at least one.

That's right, you read that correctly. Everyone has at least one.

Personal demons are personal to you because through your own negative habits, beliefs, attitudes, and fears you create them. It begins in childhood and the older you get the stronger your personal demon gets. In Romans 7 the apostle Paul complains that the things he doesn't want to do he does and the things he wants to do he doesn't. Everyone has experienced this phenomenon. It's avoiding things that are good for you and clinging on to things that are destructive. That's your personal demon manipulating you, making you a worse person inch by inch despite your desires and intentions to do better, to be better.

Personal demons unlike other demons can't be banished in a moment. It takes weeks, sometimes months, of dedicated effort to get rid of them. And once they're gone it takes a lifetime of vigilance to keep them from growing back. It requires a change of attitude, a fundamental shift in some of your beliefs about yourself and the world. Personal demons specialize in lying to us, telling us negative things until we believe them. And we allow them to do this, feed them with our own fears and paranoia. Most personal demons can be traced back to specific patterns of behavior, oftentimes even a single specific event in our childhood that helped mold us and shape us with a negative, erroneous belief.

Have you ever had these kinds of thoughts:

- I always fail.
- Why bother trying when I already know the outcome.
- I can't do that; I'm not (brave enough, smart enough, strong enough, pretty enough, etc.).
- I always mess everything up.
- Nobody loves me.
- I don't have anything of value to offer.
- I'm afraid of what will happen if I try.
- I'm afraid of embarrassing myself.

- I believe that my life can never get any better.
- I'm not anything special.
- It doesn't matter what I think.
- There has to be somebody better for the job.
- I'm a nobody.
- I'm the (dumb one, lazy one, ugly one, failure, disgrace, boring, unsuccessful one) of the family.
- I'll never amount to anything.
- I'll never succeed.
- I'll never achieve my dreams.
- I can't break this addiction.
- I ruin everything I touch.
- No one could ever love me.
- I'm too (old, young, poor, unskilled, uneducated) to (change, start something new, succeed).

These and a hundred far more personal lies are told by personal demons in an effort to keep people from becoming all God meant them to become. Every time you believe or act on a lie that your personal demon is telling you, it makes the demon stronger, it's hold firmer, and it makes it harder to break free. There is hope, though, because every personal demon no matter how large, nasty, and entrenched can be defeated.

The key to defeating a personal demon is to identify the root lie and constantly bombard it (and yourself) with the truth. Chances are your personal demon tells you several lies, the key is finding what the overall connection is. Oftentimes this overall, core lie is connected to something that happened to you as a child, an early negative experience that helped shape your personality. Maybe you learned that when you tried new things you got hurt.

Maybe you had someone tell you that you weren't smart enough. Maybe you believe that bad things happen to you and that you're helpless to stop them. Maybe you believe that you have nothing anyone wants to hear.

By spending some time in prayer, and countering each lie your personal demon tells you with a new, positive truth, you can eventually chip away at it until you find the root belief that's causing you so much trouble. As you change your belief and refuse to be manipulated, you chip away at your personal demon making it smaller and easier to defeat every time it tries to manipulate you.

You also need to visualize pulling the demon out of your abdomen. Picture it like a snake that you're trying to remove. Touch your abdomen and move your hand outward as though you were pulling out the invisible snake. Just the act can help weaken it and eventually remove it. As with most things, it is your intention, your will that it leave you, that is key. You created this thing and it's also yours to destroy. We'll discuss this more in depth in Chapter Five.

FAMILY DEMONS

Families are beautiful, wonderful, complicated things. Unfortunately, families have the ability to affect each other in intensely profound, negative ways. Whenever you go to see a new doctor they always want to know about your family history, both the physical and the psychological. Just as diseases and mental illness can run in the family, so too can negative traits and behaviors. These traits and behaviors can often be strong enough to create a family demon by much the same process as an individual creates a personal demon. This phenomenon is the origin of several well-known proverbs and possibly even where the Biblical concept of the sins of the father visiting themselves upon the children for generations comes from. We use terms like "breaking the cycle" to identify someone who has seemingly escaped a bad behavior pattern shared by multiple members of the family and even multiple generations.

Family demons are similar to personal demons except they infest entire families. Each person in the family carries around a piece of this demon. Some can carry a larger portion of it than others. Also, when one family member dies one or more of the remaining family members can "inherit" their portion. Conversely, when a child is born into a family they can receive a portion of the family demon as well. This phenomenon just adds to the perception that deaths bring despair to family and births lighten their burdens.

Everyone has the potential to be affected by family demons, but not all manifest it as intensely as they do their personal demons. It is best to go after personal demons first since they are often the stronger of the two. Also, since one demon is infecting several people a family demon is much harder to get rid of than a personal demon. There are, however, many similarities when it comes to fighting it.

First you have to identify a root negative belief or behavior that seems to affect many people in your family. This can be as obvious as alcoholism or as subtle as a pervasive sense of pessimism. Look for a behavior or a belief that multiple people share that has somehow inhibited or restricted their life in some way.

Once you have identified the negative belief or behavior and ascertained its core, now is the time to start speaking truth to it and attempt to break the pattern or cycle of bad belief or behavior. We'll discuss family demons in depth in Chapter Six.

CREATED DEMONS

Created demons are sentient demons. They have their own intelligence and their own thought. They can be created in a couple of different ways, but mostly they are created by people.

Most personal demons die with the human who created them. However, when a personal demon is particularly strong and lives inside a person for a very long time, it can eventually become so powerful that it survives the death of the person who created it. When this happens, the demon is released at death and can wonder as it likes harming and harassing anyone of the same religious background or leanings as the person who created it. It will tend to gravitate toward people with similar fears and issues as its creator. Thus, an alcoholic for example, might be tormented not just by their own personal demon and possibly a family demon but also by other demons external to themselves.

These created demons represent the vast majority of interactions people have with something they think of as demonic. People rarely notice unless they are paying attention to it the actions of personal and family demons. The sensations of being watched, of seeing things move in the corner of your eye, and intense fear are instead caused by these created demons. These are the kind you banish firmly by calling on the name of Jesus Christ and reminding them that His blood paid the price for your sins.

With these kind like tends to attract like. Created demons are more likely to harass people who have similar personal demons to the person who originally spawned the created demon. A created demon that used to live inside an alcoholic, for example, is more likely to attack somebody who already has a tendency toward alcoholism than somebody who doesn't. In essence, they are looking for a new home, one that is similar to their old home.

When this kind of demon becomes old enough and powerful enough it can move on from oppressing people to actually possessing them. Self-awareness and ability to be more cunning with its attacks grow over time as well until they can nearly, but not quite, resemble something as big and powerful as a fallen angel.

FALLEN ANGELS

These are the creatures that everyone instantly thinks of when they think of a demon. The truth is, while they are out there and actively working against God and harming humans, very few encounters with the demonic actually involve a fallen angel. These are the angels that fell from heaven with Satan. Encounters with them are fraught with great peril mainly because they are much smarter than the other types of demons and are capable of much more sophisticated, coordinated attacks. In fact, when they are present they often are commanding lesser types of demons in a very complex assault, including manipulating created, family, and personal demons.

Just because these types of demons are smarter and more powerful, though, is no reason to fear them disproportionately. Remember, all demons are subservient to God and if you resist them they must flee. When dealing with this type it is crucial that you call upon God for help immediately and that you ask Him to send angels to protect you. Command the demons to leave by the authority of Christ's blood and it is helpful to recite scriptures as well.

ALL OF THESE DEMONS ARE DEFEATABLE

You have been given power and authority by God over all these demonic forces that would seek to harm you and those you care about. That is the single most important truth that you must remember regardless of what they try to make you believe. Demons want you to feel helpless, alone, and afraid. Don't let them. We are more than conquerors through Christ.

That said, the most annoying and difficult thing about dealing with any type of demonic harassment or oppression is the amount of time it takes to fix the problem. There are short term fixes that provide immediate relief, but they are temporary. In the following chapters we will discuss each type of demon and what you can do to fight back against them, and in some cases, banish them from your life for good.

It is important to understand the role of each type of demon and what you need to do to protect yourself. However, you do not need to read the next four chapters in order. If you are experiencing any kind of physical attacks, jump straight to Chapter 7: It's Alive! Do make sure, though, that you go back and read the chapters about personal and family demons because you'll need to know that information as well and put it into practice in order to truly be free.

KEY SCRIPTURES

"And it happened on the next day that the distressing spirit from God came upon Saul, and he prophesied inside the house. So David played music with his hand, as at other times; but there was a spear in Saul's hand. And Saul cast the spear, for he said, 'I will pin David to the wall!' But David escaped his presence twice."

- I Samuel 18:10-11 (NKJV)

ACTION STEPS

- Remind yourself that God has given you authority over all demons through the shedding of Christ's blood as atonement for your sins.
- Take a deep breath and realize that you will be fighting different demons in different ways but that ultimately that blood is the key to freedom.

PRAYER OF VICTORY

God, thank You that You are above all demons and that You give me power over them. Give me discernment so that I might understand when demons are interacting with me so that I might banish them.

Chapter 5
Time to Get Personal

Personal demons, though often used as a metaphor to talk about someone's weaknesses or burdens, are very real entities. What makes them so affective and so insidious is that they are unique to each person and grown and cultivated over that person's lifetime.

The easiest way to picture them is as a snake living in your abdomen that keeps growing and becoming more powerful as you feed it. You feed it with your negativity, your bad choices, and your erroneous beliefs about yourself and the world around you. It is possible to have more than one of these, but the average person just has the one.

Personal demons are created in childhood. They are started by what I call a "trigger event". This event doesn't have to be something terrible or earth-shattering in scope. A triggering event is something that happens that you react to by creating a negative, false belief that then influences your behavior from that point forward.

Most people's negative character traits and destructive habits all stem from this personal demon and a single lie that they bought into at some point when they were a child. Possible lies include:

I am unlovable.
It is not possible to win.
New experiences are bad.
I am weak.
I always fail.

I can never do anything right.
I will never live up to my mother/father.
I am ugly.
I am stupid.
I ruin everything I touch.
No one will ever understand me.

You get the idea. This single falsehood ends up coloring our entire existence. We have learned something that just wasn't true and we end up creating behaviors based on that. This is what creates our personal demon, the thing that manipulates us throughout our lives. Eventually your personal demon becomes so big and so strong that it begins controlling you.

People use phrases like "pushing my buttons" to indicate that there are sensitive topics or areas where if someone even touches on it they are inclined to lash out instinctively, sometimes without even thinking about it. People have also noted that they do things even though they know they are bad for them and shun the things that would be good for them. The apostle Paul said "For that which I do I allow not: for what I would, that do I not; but what I hate, that do I." (Romans 7:15)

The more you feed your personal demon the more power and control it gains until you are making bad decisions right and left. Personal demons that are strong enough can even influence you to choose a life partner whose influence on you would be more negative than positive. Most personal demons die with the person who they belong to. However, some grow powerful enough that they become alive and self-aware. When this happens they can live on after their creators and are free to roam the world tormenting other people.

Even while you are alive, though, your personal demon can hurt others by manipulating you. Family, friends, coworkers, even strangers can be impacted by bad choices or hurtful words from you that were inspired by your personal demon.

Freedom from personal demons is a wonderful thing. It takes concerted effort over a period of time to attain this freedom and watchfulness afterward to maintain it, but it is well worth it.

ACCEPTING THAT YOU HAVE A PERSONAL DEMON

As with many things, the first step is admitting there is a problem. You must pray for God's guidance and the insight of the Holy Spirit to illuminate the dark corners of your mind and enable you to see yourself, your personal demon and the truth clearly.

Think about all the times when you do what you don't want to do and avoid that which you should. Think about the times when you react almost without thinking with disastrous consequences.

Acknowledge that your personal demon is an entity growing inside of you that is created by you and your life experiences and fueled by your own negative thoughts, emotions, beliefs and actions. While doing the remaining steps try and realize just how much control over your life you have given this monster. Now realize that ***you can be free of this demon*** if you are willing to be honest with yourself and do some work to make sure this demon will never control you again.

NAMING YOUR PERSONAL DEMON

Set aside some time to think about your negative behaviors, habits, and beliefs. Write them down. Chances are there are several. Try to narrow these out to a few core beliefs about yourself or the world that are negative or limiting in some way. Identify the knee-jerk negative emotions that you react with (i.e. fear, hatred, anger, jealousy, self-loathing, etc.).

Ask yourself when and where you developed these beliefs. Ask God to help you pinpoint the starting point. Odds are you will remember some event from your childhood that still irritates you in some way. It could have been when a teacher was unfair, a parent showed favoritism to a sibling, a friend hurt you.

Try to find a common connector between these emotions and the bad beliefs. (i.e. I become afraid when I think I cannot win in a certain situation and then I cease to function, I hate myself because I don't feel like I'm worth loving and no one seems to care for me, etc.). [NOTE – this step may take some time and that's okay. However, if you have real difficulty connecting the dots and boiling it all down to one thing, consider the fact that you may have more than one personal demon or that you may also have a family demon. ***IF*** you discover that you have more than one personal demon, do the work for each one.]

Now, ask yourself what the root of all of it is. What is the single controlling belief about yourself or the world that all the others fall under? What is the pattern? Identify this belief (i.e. I am invisible, my opinion doesn't matter, I don't think I can win, everything I seem to do is not enough, nobody will ever love me, I'm not good enough, God would never use me, etc.). This is THE LIE.

It might take a couple of days or weeks to figure out what the controlling, negative belief is. Keep at it until you know what THE LIE is and how the lie makes you react to situations. Narrow down your specific problem so that you can explain it in one sentence. This will be the sentence that explains your mistaken beliefs, negative emotions and bad decision making (i.e. When I'm afraid that I can't win I shut down completely). We call this THE LIE AND ITS CONSEQUENCES. Here are some more examples:

New things are bad and they frighten me so I will avoid them at all costs, choosing familiar things even if they are painful or destructive.

I am unlovable therefore I will always be alone and I push people away before they can figure out that I'm unlovable.

I am stupid so I won't even try to be good at anything since I already believe I will fail.

SPEAK TRUTH TO YOUR PERSONAL DEMON

Take the sentence that contains THE LIE AND ITS CONSEQUENCES. Address this sentence and remind yourself that the belief is a lie and the behavior is destructive. Come up with a sentence to say to combat the negative belief and destructive emotion (i.e. There is no reason to be afraid because there is always a way to win even if it takes a long time or is difficult.) This new sentence is THE TRUTH.

Choose a verse that reinforces your new sentence (i.e. If you have faith the size of a mustard seed you could tell this mountain to move and it would). Repeat THE TRUTH and the supporting verse to yourself when you get up in the morning, when you go to bed at night, and any time during the day when you are tempted to believe or act on THE LIE. You've been telling yourself THE LIE for years, so be patient but persistent with yourself while you struggle to believe and act on THE TRUTH.

Bind your personal demon every morning before you tell yourself THE TRUTH so that you weaken its influence during the day. Here are some more examples of THE TRUTH:

New experiences are a challenge that I look forward to because they help me grow and find new and better ways of doing things and new things I will enjoy.

God loves me and I have many lovable qualities and other people will recognize them.

I am smart and capable of becoming really good at something.

QUESTION YOUR MOTIVATIONS

While working to rid yourself of your personal demon, it is essential that you question your decision-making and your behaviors. Ask yourself it the things you are doing and thinking are based on THE TRUTH or THE LIE. Adjust accordingly, remembering to constantly speak THE TRUTH when tempted to act on THE LIE. Pay attention when your demon tries to push your buttons. Learn to respond instantly to the negative thought or emotion with your sentence that combats it.

Replace your old behaviors and bad decision making processes with new behaviors based on the TRUTH. If it helps, keep a log with a gold star next to every time you successfully used the new behaviors. When you use the new behavior imagine that you are kicking your personal demon in the head.

DESTROYING YOUR PERSONAL DEMON'S HOLD ON YOUR LIFE

Command your personal demon to leave you in the name of Jesus Christ whose blood was shed on the cross for your sins. Some people find that using imagery helps with this. If it helps you, imagine that you are pulling the snake from your abdomen and burning it with God's glory until even the ash is gone.

Since this is your personal demon and you've spent years growing it, it will not go away all at once. Instead you have to fight it, inch-by-inch, destroying it by pieces until you have finally vanquished it completely. This will likely take weeks if not months to accomplish. The stronger the hold it had on you, the longer it will take to break.

Every time you bind it, confront it with THE TRUTH, reject THE LIE and act on THE TRUTH you weaken it.

It's important to continue trying to cast it out. Pray that the Holy Spirit helps you with this.

FILL THE EMPTY SPACE

As you vanquish your personal demon, you need to ask the Holy Spirit to fill and heal the void that it will leave behind. If the wound that originally allowed it to grow in you is untreated and unhealed, it can spring back in a heartbeat.

DO REGULAR CHECK-UPS

You will always have a proclivity toward letting your personal demon grow back. This is why it is important to keep THE TRUTH in your heart and on your lips even after the demon is gone. It's also important to regularly examine your beliefs and behaviors and make sure that you aren't slipping back into old patterns and habits that will allow it to take root again.

KEY SCRIPTURES

"For that which I do I allow not: for what I would, that do I not; but what I hate, that do I."

- Romans 7:15

"And lest I should be exalted above measure by the abundance of the revelations, a thorn in the flesh was given to me, a messenger of Satan to buffet me, lest I be exalted above measure. Concerning this thing I pleaded with the Lord three times that it might depart from me."

- II Corinthians 12:7- (NKJV)

"'You are of your father the devil, and the desires of your father you want to do. He was a murderer from the beginning, and does not stand in the truth, because there is no truth in him. When he speaks a lie, he speaks from his own resources, for he is a liar and the father of it.'"

- John 8:44 (NKJV)

ACTION STEPS

- Acknowledge that you have a personal demon that influences you to make bad decisions.
- Every morning bind your personal demon from influencing you in the name of Jesus Christ whose blood was shed on the cross for the forgiveness of your sins.
- Identify the negative belief(s) that created your personal demon and the negative behaviors and emotions that it causes.
- Speak THE TRUTH to your personal demon every morning, every evening, and every time it presents you with THE LIE.
- Before you make decisions, stop and think about whether or not your negative belief(s) and the lies your personal demon wants you to believe are influencing them.

- Work on destroying it inch-by-inch until you are free.
- Ask the Holy Spirit to fill the void it leaves and heal you.
- Do routine check-ups to make sure it is not growing back.

PRAYER OF VICTORY

God, You have knit me together in the womb and you have seen every moment of my life and know all my scars, all my pain and fears. Show me the personal demons that I have allowed to grow inside me and help me to vanquish them for Your glory and my healing. Thank You for sending the Holy Spirit to help guide me, heal me, and free me from this demon. Thank you for giving me the victory in mind, soul, and body. Amen.

Chapter 6
Just When You Thought You Were Out...

In an individual family demons function in a very similar way to personal demons. They lead you to make bad choices through the use of negative beliefs and emotions. However, family demons have much more far-reaching impact than personal demons because they do infest entire families instead of just a single individual.

Family demons are similar to personal demons in that they live inside you and manipulate and control you, often pushing you to do things that are destructive and harmful to you or others. The biggest difference is that a family demon is actually shared by multiple people in the same family, you inherit a piece of it when you are born. This is why there are negative attributes that can be shared by several members of the same family.

Just as diseases and mental illness can run in the family, so too can negative traits and behaviors. These traits and behaviors can often be strong enough to create a family demon by much the same process as an individual creates a personal demon. This phenomenon is the origin of several well-known proverbs and it is where the Biblical concept of the sins of the father visiting themselves upon the children for seven generations comes from. We use terms like “breaking the cycle” to identify someone who has seemingly escaped a bad behavior pattern shared by multiple members of the family and even multiple generations.

Everyone has the potential to be affected by family demons, but not all manifest it as intensely as they do their personal demons. It is best to go after personal demons first since they are often the stronger of the two. Also, since one demon is infecting several people a family demon is much harder to get rid of than a personal demon. There are, however, many similarities when it comes to fighting it.

FREEING YOURSELF

Most people will only be able to focus on the part of the demon that they carry around and work to make sure that the demon and its bad behaviors don't end up affecting their own children. This is certainly the goal you should start out with. If you try to attack the entire demon at once, not only will you get intense pushback from the demon and likely other family members but you will also tire yourself out and almost certainly fail at even freeing just yourself from its influence.

As it is, you need to anticipate that just working on the piece of the family demon that you carry will agitate the whole and you might face some hostility from other family members as the pieces of the demon they carry react negatively to you. Anticipate it, pray for them, and focus on freeing yourself.

First you have to identify a root negative belief or behavior that seems to affect many people in your family including you. This can be as obvious as alcoholism or as subtle as a pervasive sense of pessimism or a fear of change. Look for a behavior or a belief that multiple people share that has somehow inhibited or restricted their life in some way. Once you have figured it out, treat the belief that triggers the behavior as THE LIE. In this regard, things are very similar to what you did when dealing with your personal demon.

Once you have identified the negative belief or behavior and ascertained its core, now is the time to start speaking THE TRUTH to it and attempt to break the pattern or cycle of bad belief or behavior. This process is just like you'd use on a personal demon. You do, however, need to be prepared for the fact that other members of the family who share this demon might try to hinder you in your efforts.

Bind this demon every morning and continue speaking THE TRUTH to it morning, evening, and throughout the day. As its hold on you weakens, focus on casting it out of yourself just like you did with the personal demon. Like the personal demon, you will be chipping away at your family demon inch-by-inch until you are free of it.

Once you do manage to eradicate the demon from yourself, remember that it is not dead. It is still living in the other members of your family. While you may be able to affect it to some extent in their lives, in order to completely destroy it will take the cooperation of your family members. This is a huge undertaking, but it can be done.

FREEING FUTURE GENERATIONS

Now that you understand what your family demon is, you can work to protect future generations from it. You must be prepared to consistently deliver to children THE TRUTH so that no matter what the other adults in their life are doing, there is someone who is not perpetuating THE

LIE. Bind the demon from affecting them on a continuous basis and pray for them daily that God will protect them from the family demon and deliver them.

When they are old enough you can explain to them how THE LIE affects members of the family and why it is a lie. Explain to them that since they know and have heard THE TRUTH from you since they were born, that they can choose to make good habits and behaviors which will help them in life.

Just as there is mention in the Bible of the sins of the father continuing on for generations, there is also discussion of God granting favor and protection to people because of a parent or relative who did as God asked. Ask God's help to make the next generations free from the burden of the family demon.

HELPING OTHERS IN YOUR FAMILY

In order to fully destroy a family demon, you need the cooperation of everyone who is carrying a piece of it. This will take education and patience on your part as you explain to them how to free themselves from its influence. This is a big job that will likely take years and a ton of prayer. Get your prayer group going on this one. As family members die off, be prepared for their portion of the demon to try and transfer to someone else. This could result in one or more family members having the demon's hold on them suddenly strengthened if they are not actively fighting against it.

Ask for the help of God and the Holy Spirit to aid you in this undertaking. Remember to continually re-examine yourself for signs of it returning and to keep educating the younger generations so that it has a chance of not manifesting in them or at least of being more quickly conquered.

This battle might last beyond you, but as long as you keep educating and praying for family members there is hope that this demon can be conquered in time and the cycle finally broken. At the very least you benefit from having it out of you so that you can make good choices instead of the bad ones it would push you toward.

KEY SCRIPTURES

"And ye shall know the truth, and the truth shall make you free."

- John 8:32 (KJV)

"You shall not bow down to them nor serve them. For I, the Lord your God, am a jealous God, visiting the iniquity of the fathers upon the children to the third and fourth generations of those who hate Me,"

- Exodus 20:5 (NKJV)

ACTION STEPS

- Determine whether you have a family demon that influences you and others in your family to make bad decisions and to be trapped in patterns of behavior.

- Every morning bind your family demon from influencing you in the name of Jesus Christ whose blood was shed on the cross for the forgiveness of your sins.
- Identify the negative belief(s) that created the family demon and the negative behaviors and emotions that it causes.
- Speak THE TRUTH to your family demon every morning, every evening, and every time it presents you with THE LIE.
- Before you make decisions, stop and think about whether or not your negative belief(s) and the lies your family demon wants you to believe are influencing them.
- Work on destroying it inch-by-inch until you are free.
- Ask the Holy Spirit to fill the void it leaves and heal you.
- Do routine check-ups to make sure it is not growing back.
- Speak THE TRUTH to the children in your family and pray for them continuously.
- Reach out to other family members and try to help them combat the influence of the family demon.

PRAYER OF VICTORY

Thank You, God, for giving me the power and the opportunity to break the cycles of the past and to escape the demons that have a hold on my family. Help this family demon to end with me and to continue on no more. Help me to share Your light and Your freedom with those members of my family who are plagued by it. Thank You for Your guidance and healing. Amen.

Chapter 7
It's Alive!

So far we've talked about personal and family demons which cause havoc in the lives of everyone. Even though these creatures exist and must be fought, they are not what most people think of when they think about demons. Whether your idea of a demon has horns and a tail or is a black shadow that shifts around the room odds are good that what you think of as demonic is a force that is external to you.

The vast majority of the creatures that torment people in a way that people think of as classically demonic are created demons. They are lesser entities than fallen angels, but they are not part of you and interactions with them are more frequent than those with fallen angels. In my thousands of encounters with external demons, only a handful have actually been fallen angels and most people will never encounter those.

That said, these created demons are sentient (thinking and self-aware) just as fallen angels are and they have all the traits commonly associated with fallen angels: malevolent intelligence, the will to do us harm, and the ability to plan and scheme and coordinate with other demons.

Created demons are formed in a variety of different ways. They can be created by fallen angels as servants or they can even be a deceased person's personal demon that was so powerful it didn't die when they did. How they were created really doesn't matter. What matters is how to get rid of them.

ARE YOU BEING HARASSED BY A DEMON?

First, you have to identify whether or not you are being harassed by a demon. Depending on the demon and depending on its purpose this harassment can be either very subtle or very overt. I will give you a list of things you can watch for, but you should know that demons are intelligent and can be very creative when tormenting someone. The better they know you and how to push your buttons the more effective they can be. You will likely experience some of the common forms of harassment but you should also be on the alert for things that are particular to you.

Nightmares

One of the sneakier ways in which demons can torment us is with nightmares. The imagery will be terrifying or disturbing but it will be designed to elicit a reaction from you. Sometimes these can be different nightmares or even the same nightmare that recurs over and over.

Halloween has always been my favorite holiday but as a little girl I had a recurring nightmare every Halloween night. The nightmare was vivid, terrifying, and each year identical in every detail. After having this nightmare for about five years in a row I told my mom about it when I didn't want to go to sleep one Halloween. She prayed with me that God would keep the nightmare away and that whatever was causing it would stop. That night I slept peacefully and even though I still remember every bit of that nightmare, I've never had it since.

I still have nightmares that are caused by demonic interference but they are always different, usually applicable to what's going on in my life spiritually at the time, and I've learned to understand them for what they are. Usually these nightmares are so vivid and so powerful that I'm able to recognize while still asleep that there is a demon messing with my mind and force myself awake in order to deal with it.

If you suffer from nightmares that seem more than usually vivid or abnormal pray before going to sleep that God will keep them at bay. You might also want to firmly banish any demon already present. If you have one of these nightmares you will certainly want to banish any demons when you wake up who might still be lingering.

Playing With Your Perceptions

Another way demons can torment you is by playing with your mind and your perceptions. Again, this can be a very subtle thing designed to set you on edge or get you to mistrust your own senses. Or, it can be so obnoxious that it becomes something that is impossible to ignore and rips your attention away from everything else. Here are a few of the things that they like to do to torment people:

- You may SEE movement out of the corner of your eyes, black shadows in the room that move around or seem out of place or darker than they should be, strange things reflected in the mirror.

- You may HEAR frightening or odd sounds, the house creaking a lot more than it usually does, things shifting or even falling over that don't seem like they should have

- You may FEEL your heart pounding, dizziness/light-headedness, chills racing up your spine, hair standing up on the back of your neck, or a presence in the room with you

- You may notice your animals or even very young children behaving with fear or avoidance. If your normally calm dog becomes agitated and starts barking at a particular spot or refuses to go into a certain room, that could be a sign that he is seeing what you're not.

Ever since I was about four, demons have loved to torment me by causing me to see movements out of the corner of my eye. They would also start to appear in mirrors, particularly bathroom mirrors late at night, until I would freak out and close my eyes. It reached the point where if I had to get up in the middle of the night to go to the bathroom I would make the entire trip with my eyes closed. Even as an adult I would avoid looking at mirrors at nighttime. It was only recently that this mirror phenomenon stopped bothering me. I felt a demon in the room with me, stopped, stared straight into the mirror and told it to show itself at its worst. It did and then I mocked it and cast it from the room. Seeing it completely was not nearly as frightening as just seeing part of it or a shadow of it as it turned out. Now mirrors hold no more terror for me.

When you do have one of these experiences it is again important to order the demonic entity out of the area using the authority of Christ's blood spilled for your sins. Two elements of that are important. The first is invoking the power of Christ and the sacrifice He made which is what freed us from sin and bondage. The second is to make sure that you say the "I" part. *I* command you to leave in the name of Jesus Christ. This is you claiming the authority Jesus gave his followers to cast out demons and taking personal responsibility for making the thing go.

It is crucial that both things are said regardless of whatever else you say when you are casting out demons. In the first half of Mark 16:17 Jesus said "And these signs shall follow them that believe; In my name shall they cast out devils" Here we see the use of Jesus' name being a necessary part. We also see that "they" cast out devils so the believers are the ones casting out the demons and they are doing it in Jesus' name. I cannot stress this point enough. You can pray to God to remove the demons from a place and He may very well do so, but eventually He will expect you to step up and learn to use the authority He has granted you.

Speaking to You

Another way in which these types of demons can harass people is far more directly. In these types of attacks you may hear voices speaking to you. Bear in mind that these types of events do not happen to everyone. If you are experiencing something like this it is imperative that you banish the demon doing it as quickly as possible. Through fear it's going to try and get you to freeze up and do nothing. You must fight back and fight back quickly.

A demon first spoke out loud to me when I was a young child and it scared me half to death. I'm still not entirely comfortable with this phenomenon because it really does startle your entire nervous system with the awareness that there is something deeply, deeply wrong. I've actually grown far more used to being touched by demons. Very few people have an experience this extreme, but I would be doing you a disservice to pretend these sorts of things never happened.

Bringing in Outside Irritants

Demons are not above using things and even other people to distract us or torment us. These attacks can range from general things that would scare most people to attacks personally targeted at you.

If you are experiencing a period of spiritual warfare and you are around other people, it is possible that demons will incite that person's personal demon to lash out at you verbally or even physically. We will discuss this type of event more fully in Chapter 10.

If you are experiencing spiritual warfare and you are around people who are possessed or heavily afflicted by demons they will very likely try to attack you. I've been chased more than once by someone whose eyes began glowing when they saw me. When this happens pray for God's protection, cast demons from the place, and get out of there as quickly as you can. I, myself, have had experience with praying, fighting, and running all at the same time.

Demons can also cause animals to torment you. I have an issue with cockroaches thanks to one of the places I've lived at that was infested. Whenever I'm having a spiritual breakthrough cockroaches show up. I've learned to see these, though, as a sign that I'm on the right path. Now the moment I see a cockroach I banish the demon who brought it around.

Physical Touching

Sad to say, I've gotten pretty used to being touched, hit, bitten, and scratched by demons. As a little girl I was nearly as afraid of being touched by a demon as I was of seeing one. However, it wasn't until I was in college that I ever experienced a physical touch.

You should know that this kind of interaction is incredibly rare and even if you have been seeing or hearing things, that doesn't mean that you will ever feel something. It is far more likely that you'll feel dread because you think you might be touched. The truth is, though, that demons rarely touch people physically. If it happens, though, it can take a variety of forms.

All that most demons can accomplish this way is something subtle, like a light tap on the shoulder when no one is there. This can be distressing because it is one of those encounters where you're trying to figure out if what just happened was real or you imagined it. This type of self-doubt and uncertainty often causes far more mental turmoil than a more solid touch so it is by far the most common.

If a demon actually bites or scratches you it might be noticeable the moment it happens or show up a couple of hours later. It is very important to keep on top of these types of injuries and keep them clean, disinfected, and make sure to apply topical antibiotics. Demons can inject toxins into your body this way. If you ignore it, it can quickly grow infected and cause you serious trouble. I ended up hospitalized and having to have surgery on one bite that I didn't take care of right away because I also had the flu and just didn't think about it too closely. It got old telling the doctors that I didn't know what had bitten me, maybe a spider or something. I have since learned to treat these kinds of injuries immediately on discovery no matter how minor they might seem at the time.

When going through times of spiritual warfare in your life it is important to also take precautions when going up and down stairs. Make sure to use handrails. I and several people that I know have been tripped or pushed down stairs by a demon. Heightened awareness of your surroundings and the potential dangers is a good thing.

One of the worst, and absolutely rarest examples of demonic touching includes a direct attack in an attempt to harm or kill you. In all my years of experience with spiritual warfare this has only happened to me once.

I was asleep and I began to have a nightmare in which I was trapped inside a car and drowning. In my dream I knew that I was being killed by a demon and that if I could only scream out for it to go away it would have to leave. I couldn't make a sound, though, because I was drowning. Still in the nightmare I finally shouted in my mind for the thing to go away in the name of Jesus Christ's blood. I felt the muscles in my throat loosen slightly. Then I woke from the nightmare.

There was a demon on top of my chest, its hands wrapped around my throat strangling me to death in the real world. Just as in the dream I couldn't say a word out loud, but I screamed the words in my mind. The thing loosened its hold on me just enough for me to repeat the words out loud and it finally vanished.

That was the first time I ever impacted a demon by saying the words in my head instead of out loud. I had never been able to put enough conviction and belief into the words without vocalizing them before. Since that day I have been able to drive out demons without speaking out loud because I understand the amount of forcefulness and belief that it takes when you are only speaking the words in your mind.

FALLEN ANGELS

So far in this chapter we've discussed what happens when you interact with a created demon. The other type of sentient demon is a fallen angel. Fallen angels are actually the type of demons that are rarest when it comes to personal encounters. When a fallen angel is present there is usually a heightened sensation of presence and intelligence. You might even see a shadowy figure. The presence of one of these creatures is usually indicative of a great amount of either physical or spiritual danger. Drop whatever you are doing and pray for protection and the assistance of angels. Then, treat it like other demons and banish it by the authority God granted you and in the name of Jesus Christ whose blood was shed on the cross for the forgiveness of your sins.

One of the problems with fallen angels is that they don't show up alone. They usually bring a horde of smaller demons with them and they can also manipulate your personal and family demons. These kinds of attacks are the ones that will drive you to your knees and have you screaming in terror or anguish. You must fight through. Silence your personal and family demons as quickly as you can so they don't distract you. Next, go after the smaller demons as they come at you, banishing each of them firmly.

If you can get help from someone else do it! The presence of this much demonic activity merits calling in the cavalry. If there's someone in the building who can help you, get their attention. If not, call someone you know and trust to help you. They can pray and they can even banish demons on your behalf. (For more on helping others see Chapter 10.)

These creatures only bother to show up if you are a threat. This means that times of intense spiritual growth or a moment when you reach a true crossroads are the times when they are most likely to show up. Most people will never encounter one of these creatures even if they are plagued by all the other types of demons.

It is important to persevere, get through the trial, and closely examine what is happening in your life that inspired one of these abominations to try and stop you from your God given destiny. If you gain attention from one of these creatures you must anticipate that you will be banishing demons on nearly an hourly basis for at least a day and maybe a lot longer. Remember this interaction accompanies a period of spiritual growth, change, and decision. Once that process is accomplished the attacks should eventually stop or at least become much more sporadic and manageable.

FIGHTING BACK

The most important thing you can do when you even suspect a demonic attack is to act instantly and decisively. Even if you're wrong and there's nothing actually there doesn't mean there won't be the next time. It's better to err on the side of caution than to risk even a minute of letting a demon run rampant through your home, work, or life.

The best method I have found to banish a demon is to say out loud "I bind any demon in this place and cast it out in the name of Jesus Christ whose blood was shed on the cross for the forgiveness of my sins. Get out now!" It is important to say this out loud if you can because it helps make it real for you and forces you to put conviction behind your words. Conviction is everything. If you don't mean what you're saying, then it has no affect. If for some reason you can't say these words out loud then you need to say them in your mind so loudly and forcefully it's as if you were shouting.

If you experience something particularly nasty or a recurrence of attacks, it's never a bad idea to secure your home. Go through every room in your home, place your hand on a wall in each room, and pray for God's protection and blessing. Pray specifically that He would send angels to guard you and your home and that He would keep the demons out. Some people like to use anointing oils to do this. Whatever makes you comfortable and helps you focus is what I would recommend. And the truth is, this is not a one-time fix. If you are being targeted, you are going to have to go through this multiple times until you make it through this period of your life. You just have to be persistent. Demons may attack you nine times, banish them ten. Do the same to your car and your office if demons are harassing you there as well.

KEY SCRIPTURES

"Be sober, be vigilant; because your adversary the devil walks about like a roaring lion, seeking whom he may devour."

- I Peter 5:8 (NKJV)

"Submit yourselves therefore to God. Resist the devil, and he will flee from you."

- James 4:7 (KJV)

"And he said to them, 'I saw Satan fall like lightning from heaven'."

- Luke 10:18 (NKJV)

ACTION STEPS

- Be on heightened alert during times of spiritual warfare and times of spiritual growth for threats from possessed people and other dangers that demons might use to their advantage.
- Pray for God's protection during times of spiritual warfare and times of spiritual growth.

- Pay attention to what is happening and ask yourself if it is natural or unnatural.
- If you see, hear, or feel anything that could be demonic, act immediately and banish any demon from the place.
- Say out loud, if at all possible, "I banish any demons that are here in the name of Jesus Christ whose blood was spilled on the cross for the forgiveness of my sins." Repeat if necessary.
- If more than one demon is coming at you at a time, get a trusted friend to help you fight them.
- During times of warfare or growth, pray and bless every room in your house as well as your car and your place of work.

PRAYER OF VICTORY

God, thank you that through you I have victory over all demons, including those that are created and the fallen angels that rebelled against you. Help me never to forget that you have already fought this battle and defeated them and that all I need to do is remind myself and them of Your victory. Protect me from all their schemes and help me be aware when I need to fight. Thank You for Your surpassing majesty and power and the authority over them that you have granted me. Amen.

Chapter 8
The Battle Belongs to the Lord, But You Still Need to Arm Yourself

God has already defeated Satan. The enemy's fate is sealed. God is portrayed as our rock, our shield and our deliverer (Psalm 18:2). However, that doesn't mean that we can sit idly by while spiritual warfare is raging around us.

The Bible tells us that we are wrestling with things not of this earth and instructs us to put on the full armor of God (Ephesians 6:11-17). These are tools to help you fight and to keep you focused and calm while doing so. I'll discuss some of these tools as well as others I have found useful in spiritual warfare.

SCRIPTURE AND TRUTH

Scripture is referenced as the sword of the Spirit. That's because it is the ultimate TRUTH and demons cannot stand against it. When under spiritual attack it's important to know scripture not only to shout at the enemy but also to calm yourself and maintain your resolve.

It is important to remember the greatness of God and the promises He has made to us. Jesus, when he was tempted by Satan, responded with scripture. There is no argument Satan can use to countermand scripture. Our own logic he can poke holes in. We must renew our minds and bolster ourselves by remembering the promises of God.

The Bible instructs us to gird our waists with truth. We are also told that the truth sets us free (John 8:32). In learning to fight your personal and family demons you worked on speaking THE TRUTH whenever they try to sell you on a lie. The truth is a powerful thing that can uphold and sustain us, guard us and protect us. Yes, even free us. Here are some truths you need to keep in mind.

- God has promised never to leave us or forsake us no matter how dark things might get. He will be with us always. (Matthew 28:20)
- All things will work together for your good because you love the Lord and have been called to His service. (Romans 8:28)
- God has already defeated Satan.
- God will not allow us to go through anything we can't handle. (I Corinthians 10:13)

FAITH

Faith combats fear and triumphs over doubt. The Bible instructs us to take up the shield of faith which quenches the fiery darts of the devil. That's because fear and doubt are the two things demons constantly bombard us with. Faith keeps us going when nothing else can.

You must have faith that God will help you, guide you, and bring you through this time of spiritual warfare. You must believe that with all your soul so that you don't become overly frightened or discouraged and risk stumbling. When you feel yourself beginning to doubt, ask

God to reinforce your faith and focus on the promises he has made and the TRUTH that you know.

SONGS OF PRAISE AND VICTORY

Create a playlist of songs that make you feel the power of God and His victory over darkness. Music is a powerful tool and used against the enemy it is also a weapon. The Bible tells us that a demon fled from Saul when David played songs of praise on the harp. Songs that praise God and proclaim His victory hurt demons and are hated by them. Here are a few of my personal favorites:

The Battle Hymn of the Republic
Our God is an Awesome God
The Battle Belongs to the Lord
Onward Christian Soldiers
Via Dolorosa
He's Alive by Dolly Parton
Creed by Petra
This Blood by Carman
Jericho by Carman

Create playlists for yourself but also memorize a few songs and hymns that you can sing yourself when you need to.

MEMORIES OF PAST VICTORIES

In the Old Testament it was common for people to recount the wondrous things God had done for them or their ancestors, particularly before going into a battle or asking Him to move again on their behalf. Reminding yourself of the times that God has helped you be victorious reassures you that it has happened before and will happen again. It also reminds the enemy of his past defeats. It also serves as a way to connect with God through recounting the shared history of your relationship and reminding Him that you are relying on Him now as you have in the past.

When things get dark or hard it's important to remember that God has seen you through tough times before. If this is your first time experiencing spiritual warfare (or at least being aware that you are) you can still recall the times when God has helped you in other circumstances and you have prevailed over difficulties that stood in your way.

You can even take a page from those early children of God and recount victories that God gave to your parents, your grandparents, and so forth. This reinforces to you and the demons you are fighting that you are one of God's cherished children and that He will aid you in battle.

KEY SCRIPTURES

"Put on the whole armor of God, that you may be able to stand against the wiles of the devil. For we do not wrestle against flesh and blood, but against principalities, against powers, against the rulers of the darkness of this age, against spiritual *hosts* of wickedness in the heavenly *places*. Therefore take up the whole armor of God, that you may be able to withstand in the evil day, and having done all, to stand. Stand therefore, having girded your waist with truth, having put on the breastplate of righteousness, and having shod your feet with the preparation of the gospel of peace; above all, taking the shield of faith with which you will be able to quench all the fiery darts of the wicked one. And take the helmet of salvation, and the sword of the Spirit, which is the word of God;"

- Ephesians 6:11-17 (NKJV)

"But he stood in the midst of the ground, and defended it, and slew the Philistines: and the Lord wrought a great victory."

-II Samuel 23:12 (KJV)

"'teaching them to observe all things that I have commanded you; and lo, I am with you always, even to the end of the age. Amen."

- Matthew 28:20 (NKJV)

"And ye shall know the truth, and the truth shall make you free."

- John 8:32 (KJV)

"No temptation has overtaken you except such as is common to man; but God is faithful, who will not allow you to be tempted beyond what you are able, but with the temptation will also make the way of escape, that you may be able to bear it." - I Corinthians 10:13 (NKJV)

"The Lord is my rock and my fortress and my deliverer; My God, my strength, in whom I will trust; My shield and the horn of my salvation, my stronghold."
- Psalm 18:2 (NKJV)

"And we know that all things work together for good to those who love God, to those who are the called according to His purpose."
- Romans 8:28 (NKJV)

ACTION STEPS

- Make a list of scriptures that speak TRUTH to you and help bolster your faith.
- Memorize those scriptures and repeat them to yourself on a daily basis.
- Make yourself a playlist of songs that speak of God's victory and His faithfulness and anything else that makes you confident in your ability to conquer evil in His name.
- Memorize a few songs of praise that you can sing when you need to.
- Make yourself a list of past victories that God has brought about in your life. If you want add in victories that He brought about in the lives of your ancestors as well.
- Review that list whenever you are going into battle.

PRAYER OF VICTORY

God, thank You for giving me the tools to protect myself and to defeat Satan and his minions at every turn. Thank you for being my Rock and my Deliverer. Help me to stand strong in your promises and not falter. Thank You for granting me victory over the darkness just as you have granted me numerous victories in the past. Amen.

Chapter 9
Natural Situations, Supernatural Interference

Demons can be creative and can do all kinds of things to irritate and distract you. That said, if they can accomplish that through just a little effort they will. They don't always create unique problems. Sometimes they just aggravate existing ones. Demons love to pile on and make anything you're experiencing worse. To that end they often take advantage of otherwise natural situations. These can include physical, mental, financial or relationship problems.

Let me take a moment right here to stress something. If you have <u>any</u> sort of physical or psychological problem, see your doctor! Ninety-nine percent of the time any problems you have will be <u>completely</u> natural. Even in that one percent of the time when they might not be, it is still important to seek medical or psychological treatment for any problems you are experiencing.

Demons attack us to discourage us and keep us from living our best lives and accomplishing God's will for us. Compounding problems that we have is one of the quickest ways to occupy our time and energy.

PHYSICAL PROBLEMS

Most people have some sort of physical ailment that they are prone to. This might be headaches, muscle tension, stomach trouble, etc. Chances are, these problems occupy a good deal of your thoughts when they are present and active. If you notice a change in the frequency or intensity of physical ailments see your doctor and check to see if a demon could be aggravating it.

For me allergies have been a problem all of my life. They can become unbearable at times. Over the years I've learned what medications to take and what allergens to avoid in order to manage my allergies. That said, there are days where they flare for absolutely no reason I can figure out. When this happens, my nose will run uncontrollably and I will be incredibly stuffed up as well making me fuzzy-headed. When it gets bad like this I am incapable of working.

One day when this happened I realized that it was the worst possible timing and there was no obvious cause. I stopped and actually tried to cast out any demon that might be harassing my sinuses and stirring up my allergies. Within five minutes my sinuses cleared, my nose stopped running, and I was able to do the important work I had scheduled for that day.

Now, when I have allergies and can't find a physical reason, I stop and check to see if I'm being harassed by a demon. At least twenty-five percent of the time there is a demon aggravating my allergies. I know a woman who has to do the same thing when she gets migraines multiple days in a row. She is prone to migraines and has struggled with them for decades, but when they come too frequently it's often a sign of demonic interference and can be cleared up by getting rid of the demon that's stirring up trouble.

When wondering if a demon is aggravating an existing physical ailment (or even in the rare instances where they are causing a new one) stop and ask yourself what this trouble is keeping you from doing, thinking, or praying that you would otherwise be doing if it wasn't sapping your energy, strength, time, physical ability, or focus. If you would be doing something important, it could be that you have an unwelcome visitor stirring up trouble. If you have been experiencing a period of spiritual warfare you should question anything unusual or excessive that happens to you and order any demons that are harassing you to leave.

PSYCHOLOGICAL AND EMOTIONAL PROBLEMS

Depression, stress, anxiety, anger, and sadness are all emotions naturally experienced by humans that are dependent on a number of factors including life circumstances and hormones. Emotions are a natural part of existence. It's when they become excessive, all-consuming, or destructive that they become a problem. Most of the time this is something that can be fixed or controlled through medication, therapy, or a combination of the two.

Occasionally, though, demons will manipulate your mental and emotional state to their own ends. Excessive depression, anxiety, despair, and anger are some of their favorite targets. This is because these emotions distract and keep a person from doing what they should be doing. Intensity of these emotions can even lead people to try and hurt themselves or others.

If someone has wronged you, it is natural to feel angry. If the wrong is slight and the anger you feel is wildly out of proportion you might have a problem. If you feel the need to hurt them then there could be a demon interfering with you spiking the natural anger until it is unnatural in its intensity. The demon could be trying to push you into doing something you shouldn't or keep you from doing what you should.

As with physical problems it is always important to seek medical advice when experiencing mental and emotional problems. If known existing problems spike out of control it's important to return to your doctor and update them about the situation. It could be a good idea, though, to just check and make sure there isn't a demon "helping" to make things worse.

WHEN IT ALL GOES WRONG

You've probably heard the expression, "It never rains, but it pours." Sometimes it seems that when one thing goes wrong that it sets off a chain reaction in our lives and everything goes wrong. Sometimes this just happens. Sometimes everything goes right, too.

However, when there seems to be an increasingly disproportionate number of things going wrong, it's a good idea to bind any demons that might be causing you trouble. Take a look at the life of Job. In practically the blink of an eye he lost his wealth, his family, everything. We know from scriptures that those losses were Satan tormenting and testing him to see if he would remain true to God.

As believers we are not promised perfect lives. We are, however, promised that everything will work for our good. This is true even if we don't see how. That doesn't mean, though, that we just ignore the enemy if he is attacking us. We must fight back. If there are an inordinate number of things going wrong, bind and cast out any demons that might be at the heart of it.

SOMETIMES IT ISN'T EVEN ABOUT YOU

When you have learned to defend yourself from demonic attacks you will find that the enemy begins to try new tactics. Sometimes they'll come at you through a friend, a loved one, or a coworker. By manipulating that person into hurting you in some way they can get to you and cause you to lose the peace and persistence with which you have been dealing with your problems.

On the flip side of that you need to be aware that sometimes demons harass you not because they are trying to get at you but because they are trying to get at someone else. To that end we need to learn to mind our tongues like it warns us to in scriptures (Proverbs 12:18, Psalm 34:13). The angry, hurtful, or careless thing we say to someone else may be a terrible blow to that other person that the demons are planning on using to their advantage. In that case you are being used as a weapon. Lives have been shattered, friendships have been destroyed, and families have been torn apart by the wrong word at the wrong time.

It's on us, then, to monitor our words and actions closely when they stray into the negative realm and make sure that what we're saying or doing is what we want to be and not a suggestion from a demonic influence.

You should also be aware that if someone else is being hurtful to you that it might be that demons, particularly their own personal ones, are trying to push you away so that you will be in no position to help them later. Demons work overtime to isolate people from those most willing and able to help them. We will discuss this further in Chapter 10.

KEY SCRIPTURES

"And behold, there was a woman who had a spirit of infirmity eighteen years, and was bent over and could in no way raise herself up. But when Jesus saw her, He called her to Him and said to her, 'Woman, you are loosed from your infirmity.' And He laid His hands on her, and immediately she was made straight, and glorified God. ... So ought not this woman, being a daughter of Abraham, whom Satan has bound—think of it—for eighteen years, be loosed from this bond on the Sabbath?'"

- Luke 13:11-13,16 (NKJV)

"There is one who speaks like the piercings of a sword, But the tongue of the wise promotes health."

- Proverbs 12:18 (NKJV)

"Keep your tongue from evil, And your lips from speaking deceit."

- Psalm 34:13 (NKJV)

ACTION STEPS

- Identify if there is a problem that is keeping you from doing something important.

- Cast out any demons who may be causing or aggravating that problem in the name of Jesus Christ whose blood was shed on the cross for the forgiveness of your sins.
- Pay attention to the things that stop you from doing important tasks or from doing work God wants you to do.
- Pray for God's healing and be vigilant to cast out demons who might try to take advantage of existing problems.

PRAYER OF VICTORY

Thank You God that You are Lord over everything, both the natural things of this world and the supernatural. I ask for Your protection and blessings in every area of my life and that You would guard my health, my finances, and my relationships and keep the enemy from them. Thank You that through You I have victory over everything, including death and that I will dwell with You in eternity. Protect those I care about when I'm not there to watch over them and keep Satan and his minions from them. Amen.

Chapter 10
When It's Time to Call in the Cavalry

I've been under demonic attack countless times in my life, but I've also been called on a lot to help others who are experiencing demonic attacks. All of us who go through this need help at some point or another either because we're too blind to see what's happening or we're too overwhelmed with negative emotions to fight back or because we're simply outnumbered and feeling like we're being overrun.

Sometimes when you're faced with a large problem and the fear of failure is crushing you, you might need to get help from some prayer warriors, friends who understand what you're going through, or spiritual advisers that you trust. It's perfectly okay to ask for help. You can have trusted friends pray for you and even help fight for you. I have a small circle of friends who I know will do this for me at the drop of a hat. Just as they know I will do the same for them.

IT'S OKAY TO ASK FOR HELP

Everyone needs help sometimes. This is true in life and it's true in spiritual warfare. It's okay to ask for someone else's help fighting battles. This is not a failure or weakness on your part, it is simply a smart, tactical move. Most of the time you should be able to fight by yourself. If you never fight by yourself, then you should be concerned and learn to trust and push yourself a bit more. However, as long as you have and can fight on your own you don't need to feel bad when calling in reinforcements. When you are learning or tired or faced with big trouble it's natural to want someone at your side.

I have asked for help from others numerous times. The most common type of help I request is prayer. I ask people to pray for me that I am safe, that my family is safe, that I am focused, that God sends angels to battle with me or for me, and that I have strength enough for the entire battle. I have spent up to an hour at a time engaged in continuous warfare and that is exhausting both mentally and physically.

Think about the emotional and spiritual torment Jesus endured in the Garden of Gethsemane. He was in such distress he was actually sweating blood. He took three of his closest friends with him to the Garden and asked them to watch and pray while He struggled with the task at hand. I think this is a fantastic example of how to use friends as prayer support when you are fighting your own battles.

Sometimes I ask for confirmation of what it is that I'm sensing. I'm most likely to do this when I'm extremely tired or distracted or I'm just wanting to be stubborn and am trying not to admit to myself that there is a supernatural cause to the problem at hand.

Sometimes I ask for help when I am too busy dealing with a different demon or another problem and there is an immediate spiritual need. This is when I will call on a trusted friend and ask them to help someone else.

SOME WARFARE REQUIRES MULTIPLE WARRIORS

There are some battles that are so big you really need to call in extra troops. This is especially true if you encounter a fallen angel. They are rarely seen, but if they show up they usually bring a host of lesser demons with them. This type of onslaught can overwhelm even a seasoned warrior.

When battling demons that are plaguing someone else it can also be helpful to get someone else to assist you. You can take turns fighting and watching to see what the response is.

FIND PEOPLE YOU TRUST

In any battle you need to be able to trust the people fighting beside you. The same is true with spiritual warfare. I have a few close, handpicked friends whom I can call on to help me when I'm facing spiritual warfare. Some of them I've helped teach how to fight and all of us have learned and grown together over the years. I trust the judgment and value their insights and opinions. All of them are willing and able to tell me the truth about a situation even if I don't want to hear it. I also know that I can call on each of them and they will drop everything to fight, pray, or offer advice.

When choosing your own team look for people who will support you and pray for you no matter what. Look for people who can be trusted because they will see you when you are vulnerable and they will be the ones to keep you accountable as you battle your own personal and family demons.

LEARN TO SPEAK THE SAME "LANGUAGE"

When dealing with the spiritual realm some people can more accurately visualize what is happening than others. When you have a warfare partner, make sure that you understand the types of descriptions and imagery they will be using to reference the experience and vice versa. This cuts down on confusion and the need for explanation when you are actively involved in fighting.

With one of my prayer partners we use the terms PD and FD to refer to Personal Demons and Family Demons respectively. If we just say the word "demon" we both know we're referencing an external, created demon. These distinctions become important when you're both working to help someone else. A sentence might go something like this, "I'm trying to get rid of the demon in the corner but his PD keeps trying to lash out at me. Can you do something about the PD?"

BE RESPECTFUL

Don't call in the cavalry for every tiny little interaction. Your friends need time to fight their own battles and attend to their life needs. Instead, call on them when you are feeling overwhelmed or have multiple demons to battle or feel that you are at a crossroads. Understand that sometimes it's just enough to have them praying for you and knowing that you are going through something.

Don't be shy about asking for help, but don't overwhelm others when you don't actually need the help. The more you grow accustomed to spiritual warfare the easier it will be to understand which situations require the prayer or intervention of others.

KEY SCRIPTURES

"Then Jesus came with them to a place called Gethsemane, and said to the disciples, 'Sit here while I go and pray over there.' And He took with Him Peter and the two sons of Zebedee, and He began to be sorrowful and deeply distressed. Then He said to them, 'My soul is exceedingly sorrowful, even to death. Stay here and watch with Me.' He went a little farther and fell on His face, and prayed, saying, 'O My Father, if it is possible, let this cup pass from Me; nevertheless, not as I will, but as You will.' Then He came to the disciples and found them sleeping, and said to Peter, 'What? Could you not watch with Me one hour? Watch and pray, lest you enter into temptation. The spirit indeed is willing, but the flesh is weak.'"

- Matthew 26:36-41 (NKJV)

"Though one may be overpowered by another, two can withstand him. And a threefold cord is not quickly broken."

- Ecclesiastes 4:12 (NKJV)

ACTION STEPS

- Find one or two people you can trust that have had experience with spiritual warfare or at least have had encounters with demons.
- Get on the same page with those people in terms of what you call demons, the imagery you use, etc.
- Call one of those people when you feel completely overwhelmed by the demonic or need a second opinion about a potentially demonic situation.
- Be willing to help them just as they help you.
- Remember that the Holy Spirit can help you fight.

PRAYER OF VICTORY

Thank You, God, that I don't have to be alone in this fight. Send me the people I need to help me that I can trust. Thank You that Your Holy Spirit will fight on my behalf and let me remember to ask for His help. Amen.

Chapter 11
What to Do When You Are the Cavalry

It's one in the morning and the phone rings. On the other end is a person who is scared and upset and looking to you for help. Someone you know is under demonic attack and they're reaching out to you because they don't know what else to do. They know it's the middle of the night. They're desperate and relieved that you answered because they're seeing things or hearing things and going out of their mind with fear.

I've fielded my share of middle of the night phone calls. I've even made a few myself. The important thing to do is to stay calm and focus on the problem. You need to help the person on the other end of the line calm down and get control of the situation so both of you can get some sleep.

Demons can attack at any time of the day or night. However, their preferred time to strike is at night. Why? There are many reasons. Chiefly because most people are still afraid of the dark and what they can see on some level. Also, people feel more isolated and cut off from others during the middle of the night. Plus, there are fewer distractions, and demons can get someone's undivided attention quickly and easily. Finally, if they can interrupt your sleep schedule they can get you more and more off-balance to the point where you're making poor choices based out of exhaustion.

Ninety percent of the time or more someone will reach out to you for help with the demonic when they are being attacked by created demons. Only very self-aware people who are well on the path to victory will ask for help when dealing with a personal or family demon.

Of course, not everyone who needs your help will know what is happening to them. They might start talking about things they've been experiencing or overwhelming feelings that are dragging them down. However they come to you, you have found yourself in the position of their support network as they fight through this time in their lives.

WHAT DOES IT MEAN TO BE THE CAVALRY?

When someone asks you for help the first thing you should do is pray that God sends angels to protect both them and you. You should be prepared to be attacked yourself while helping someone else. It may not happen, but be ready just in case. Here it is important to know that all demons, no matter what kind, are subject to the authority of God. He has therefore granted you authority over all of them. If your friend is a Christian, an agnostic, a Wiccan, a Buddhist, it doesn't matter. You can still help. The farther removed their religion is from Christianity the less effective your normal efforts will be but they still have an impact. God and his angels interact on every plane with every soul regardless of their belief structure. Call in God and ask for angelic help in extra doses when your friend is not a Christian. The important thing here is your faith and your belief that you can affect the spiritual realm and make things better for the other person.

Ideally you will help out until your friend gets their second wind or can start thinking clearly without having their mind messed with and can start fighting for themselves. In nasty situations, particularly those involving multiple demons, it might take both your efforts to bring a modicum of peace for a few hours or a few days.

If you step in to help once, expect that you will have to do so more than once until your friend becomes more confident and competent at fighting the demons on their own. I have had my share of 4 am calls where I had to wake up and help someone. The good news is that with help and encouragement most people can learn to stand on their own and those 4 am calls will stop. Patience and persistence are key. And never hesitate to call in other people for help if the job seems too intense. I've had experiences where it took 5 people who knew what they were doing to kill a single, powerful demon. If that's what it takes, don't hesitate to ask your friends and prayer partners for help, or at the very least, prayer for you as you're going through it.

LISTEN WITHOUT TRYING TO RATIONALIZE

This can be especially difficult to do, regardless of whether you've had direct contact with the demonic or not. A lot of people believe that those of us who acknowledge that the demonic exists find Satan everywhere, hiding under every rock so to speak. The reality is, most of the time we try to find any other explanation except for the demonic. Dealing with the demonic can be a strain emotionally, mentally, and physically. Therefore, it's human nature to want to find an easier explanation. A thousand natural explanations will spring to your lips.

"You're just depressed, it's normal this time of the year."

"Your money is coming. Sometimes the post office takes days longer than it should. Who knows why? It just happens."

"It's an old house, of course it makes lots of noises."

"You just tripped on the stairs. You should be more careful."

"That guy who chased you was probably just a mugger hoping to snatch your purse."

"Just because the doctors can't figure out what's wrong with you doesn't mean anything. More specialists will figure it out."

And sometimes it *is* just depression, a foul up with the mail, an old house settling, a stubbed toe, a mugger, or a tricky diagnosis. I've said something similar to most of these things to people when I didn't want to admit that there might be something supernatural going on instead.

Human beings have a natural need to soothe those they care for. Calming them down and helping them to find rational explanations is what we do all the time. Oftentimes the harder struggle is to listen objectively to what the other person has to say, examine the evidence, and if it seems likely make the suggestion that they might have a supernatural problem on their hands.

SEEK OUT BOTH NATURAL AND SUPERNATURAL REMEDIES

The truth is we should all act as though there is a natural solution and a supernatural one. Encourage your friend to seek medical and psychological help. Urge them to get the rickety handrail on their staircase fixed. Tell them not to walk alone in dark places where they are likely to encounter criminals waiting to take advantage of them.

Don't stop there, though. Seek out any possible supernatural cause and safeguard against it. Help them understand how to cast out demons who are harassing them, introduce them to the concepts of personal and family demons who can impact their decision making processes and cause them to make bad choices or even stumble on a staircase.

The truth is, there may be no supernatural element at work in whatever it is that is happening to them. However, there might also be no natural element at work in whatever is happening to them. More times than not, though, it is a combination of natural and supernatural. Demons are opportunistic creatures. Why create a brand new problem when you can take advantage of one that already exists?

In the case of people with mental illness people have asked me which I think comes first, demonic affliction or mental illness. The truth is, it doesn't matter. Where there is mental illness there is opportunity for demonic affliction without discovery. It doesn't always happen, but it is like an open door invitation. Where there is demonic affliction if left unchecked mental illness will surely follow. You need to make sure people get the help they need on both levels.

TEACH THE TOOLS THAT HAVE WORKED FOR YOU

If someone is looking to you for help it's because they believe that you have knowledge or skill that they don't. Sometimes you do, sometimes you just know as much as they do. What's happening here is that the demonic affliction they are experiencing is making them unsure of themselves and they feel helpless. They're looking to you to be the strong one, to remind them what to do and to help them when they can't help themselves.

In college my one roommate and I had been under pretty intense demonic attack for months. Mostly they would attack my roommate and I would cast them out of our room. She was new to the whole process in comparison to me. One night the demons turned their sights on me and I was frozen with terror. I knew what to do, but suddenly I didn't feel like I could. I called out to my roommate and told her what was happening and asked for her help. She went after those demons with a vengeance! It was the night she learned to truly fight.

Even seasoned fighters need help from time to time when they're feeling overwhelmed or exhausted or confused. Sometimes even I can't tell if I'm under demonic attack or I'm just experiencing a series of crappy events or unhealthy emotions. That's when I reach out to those I know and trust, some of whom I helped train, to get their opinion on my situation. When you're too close to the problem a second opinion can be invaluable.

CLAIM THE VICTORY FOR THEM

Every word you speak on behalf of someone else when it comes to spiritual warfare has two purposes. The first is to drive out the demons attacking them. The second is to encourage them. Claim their victory over the demons in the name of Christ. Praise God in prayer or song. You are working to restore their equilibrium that the demons have taken from them. The sooner you can do this, the sooner you can both rest.

The more you work to encourage them and show them how to fight, the sooner they will stand up for themselves.

GET THEM INVOLVED

Oftentimes people can do what they thought they couldn't if they know someone is there with them. Think of this as hand-holding. Do what you need to in order to calm the worst of the demonic attack and then encourage them to take it the rest of the way. Get them to bind and cast out the demons in Jesus' name. They need to get used to doing this and the first few times it's easier when someone you trust is there to back you up. Soon they should be able to do it on their own without calling you in the middle of the night.

BE PREPARED TO BE ATTACKED YOURSELF

When someone you know is under demonic attack, the demons will do whatever they can to keep help from arriving. Therefore, don't be surprised if the afflicted person lashes out at you. It might seem like they are pushing you away.

Most of the time it's not them, but the demons that are tormenting them who precipitated that action. The heavier the assault someone is under the less they are thinking straight and the more their personal demon can control and manipulate them.

You have to let the things they say and do roll off of you. If you get angry or hurt and attack back, you are just playing into the hands of the enemy. If you have not 100% vanquished your own family and personal demons this could be incredibly difficult, especially if you've known the other person for a while or are very close. It is possible for your personal demon and their personal demon to start acting together to drive you apart. It will be as though every button that can be pushed will be and it will drive both of you deeper and deeper into a dark place and farther and farther apart from each other.

You must be prepared for attacks that will hit close to home. Bind your own personal and family demons and think very carefully before you speak. Remember, this is not about you and your feelings and your ego. This is about helping the other person. The cavalry does not fire on the people it's trying to rescue but fires on the enemy.

This is going to require a lot of prayer and faith and patience on your part and a commitment not to be drawn into a battle with the other person, regardless of your own history with them.

HELPING EVEN WHEN YOU HAVEN'T BEEN ASKED

Sometimes in old movies the cavalry came riding to the rescue even if the people under attack hadn't been able to send word that they needed help. If you get an intense urge to pray for someone or you notice that something is happening to them, you need to help. Evil prevails when good men do nothing.

The Declaration of Independence states: "But when a long train of abuses and usurpations, pursuing invariably the same Object evinces a design to reduce them under absolute Despotism, it is their right, it is their duty, to throw off such Government, and to provide new Guards for their future security." I like the modern translation given by the hero in the film *National Treasure*. He says, "It means if there's something wrong those who have the ability to take action have the responsibility to take action".

I have the ability to help people fight their demons. I have the responsibility to help people fight their demons. That is an awesome and terrible thought all at the same time. The truth is, though, once you have tasted freedom, you want it for everyone else.

However, you cannot force someone else to believe that demons exist or that they are being attacked by them. (For a discussion about talking about the demonic with others see Chapter 12.) If they won't that makes your job harder, but there are still things you can do to help.

You do not need a person's permission to cast out created demons that are afflicting them. These are subject to you by the authority given you by Christ. It doesn't matter if they're coming after you, your neighbor, or the stranger five seats away from you in the movie theater. You can cast them out.

As always, this is not going to be a one-time process. You will have to do it repeatedly, and eventually for any kind of semi-permanent solution you will probably need the cooperation of the person they are going after. Hopefully, though, your efforts and God's efforts to get through to them will bear fruit and they will reach a place where they can listen and participate.

Demons flourish because people are afraid to share their experiences with each other. Be someone who is open not only to talking about what you've faced but also to hearing about other people's issues in this area. The more we talk about it, the more we help each other, the more we shine a light in the darkness that forces Satan and his minions to flee.

Also, don't be afraid to tell friends if you think they are under spiritual attack. Some people don't know the signs. Others are too wrapped up in their own heads to stop and think clearly and recognize what is really happening to them. There can be a lot of medical, psychological, and social reasons for changes in people's behaviors. Those avenues should always be explored thoroughly. However, here are some signs to look for when trying to determine if someone you care for is under demonic oppression.

- Sudden loss of interest in spiritual matters
- Personality changes for the negative
- Attempts at self-injury or suicide

- Sudden lack of care for their physical appearance
- Panic attacks, sustained depression, despair
- Violent mood swings, unpredictable behavior, paranoia
- Inability to cope with day-to-day life
- Engaging in behaviors or sins that would normally be abhorrent to them
- Reckless disregard for their own safety
- Isolating from those who love them and could help them

Again, common sense has to play into this. Check for other factors in their life that could be causing these symptoms and encourage them to get the help they need. Oftentimes spiritual attack can either trigger or be aggravated by other conditions. Satan doesn't attack us where we are strong but where we are weak. He goes after the chinks in our armor.

SEEING WITH THE EYES OF YOUR SPIRIT

You don't have to be in the same room with someone to help them. You can be on opposite ends of the earth with no contact with them and still help. Picture that person and what you know of their location as best you can. Think about them really hard.

Then do the same thing you would do for yourself. Bind, rebuke, and cast out any demons affecting that other person in the name of Jesus Christ whose blood was shed on the cross for both your sins. Imagine that the demons are flies hovering around your friend and think of yourself swatting them away. You can do this in person, on the phone, or even without any contact with your friend whatsoever. Your intention, your taking responsibility for banishing the demons harassing them in Christ's name is what is important here.

WHEN CHILDREN ARE BEING AFFLICTED

Children are known for having incredibly active imaginations. Unfortunately this can sometimes lead to adults being dismissive of things children say when they shouldn't be. Everyone wants children to live happy, stress-free lives for as long as possible free of excessive fear and bad memories. However, children must also be protected. They are imaginative and because the world is so new to them they are often far more receptive to the parts of it that adults have been trained to block out.

The bottom line is, if your child tells you that there's a monster hiding under their bed or in their closet, GO AND CHECK! You can do this without overly alarming the child, but don't dismiss their concerns out of hand. If they are truly afraid there is the very real possibility that they have reason to be.

One of the best things you can do is introduce your child to God's loving protection and help them pray to Him to make the monsters go away. Teach them to tell the monsters to go away. You don't even have to use words like "demon" if you're not ready to talk to your child about that aspect of the world yet. Trust me, though, every child instinctually understands that there are bad things out there. Telling your child there are no such things or just to ignore it won't make them feel safer.

Demons started coming after me when I was very, very young. They talked to me, they appeared to me, and they tormented me with recurring nightmares. My mother helped me banish the demon that was causing the nightmares by praying with me to God to keep that specific nightmare from ever returning. It never did. Three-and-a-half decades later I still remember that nightmare in vivid detail. Just as vividly I remember my mom praying with me that it would stop coming to me and I remember my immense relief the next morning when I woke up without having it. That freedom was one of the greatest gifts she ever gave me.

Your child can't prove to you that there is a monster hiding in their closet or under their bed. They don't know yet how to protect themselves from the supernatural. It is up to you to comfort but not trivialize and to make sure that your child isn't the victim of systematic demonic attack.

I'm not the only one I know who experienced demonic attack as a child. A friend was nearly killed as a small girl when a demon threw her down a staircase. God had big plans for her, though, and there was an angel at the bottom who caught her.

Demons can aggressively target children whom God has chosen to do great things. They want to usurp God's plan for that person's life. For me, they tried to make me so terrified of demons that I would never fight back, never talk about them, never help others to do the same. The plan backfired. Because of the torment that I experienced I have grown determined not to let others suffer in darkness and fear the way that I did.

KEY SCRIPTURES

"But the Spirit of the Lord departed from Saul, and a distressing spirit from the Lord troubled him. And Saul's servants said to him, 'Surely, a distressing spirit from God is troubling you. Let our master now command your servants, who are before you, to seek out a man who is a skillful player on the harp. And it shall be that he will play it with his hand when the distressing spirit from God is upon you, and you shall be well.' So Saul said to his servants, 'Provide me now a man who can play well, and bring him to me.' ... And so it was, whenever the spirit from God was upon Saul, that David would take a harp and play it with his hand. Then Saul would become refreshed and well, and the distressing spirit would depart from him."
- I Samuel 16:14-17, 23 (NKJV)

"And he began to teach them, that the Son of man must suffer many things, and be rejected of the elders, and of the chief priests, and scribes, and be killed, and after three days rise again. And he spake that saying openly. And Peter took him, and began to rebuke him. But when he had turned about and looked on his disciples, he rebuked Peter, saying, Get thee behind me, Satan: for thou savourest not the things that be of God, but the things that be of men."

- Mark 8:31-33 (KJV)

"Then Jesus came with them to a place called Gethsemane, and said to the disciples, 'Sit here while I go and pray over there.' And He took with Him Peter and the two sons of Zebedee, and He began to be sorrowful and deeply distressed. Then He said to them, 'My soul is exceedingly sorrowful, even to death. Stay here and watch with Me.' He went a little farther and fell on His face, and prayed, saying, 'O My Father, if it is possible, let this cup pass from Me; nevertheless, not as I will, but as You will.' Then He came to the disciples and found them sleeping, and said to Peter, 'What? Could you not watch with Me one hour? Watch and pray, lest you enter into temptation. The spirit indeed is willing, but the flesh is weak.'"

- Matthew 26:36-41 (NKJV)

"Though one may be overpowered by another, two can withstand him. And a threefold cord is not quickly broken."

- Ecclesiastes 4:12 (NKJV)

"A friend loves at all times, And a brother is born for adversity."

- Proverbs 17:17 (NKJV)

ACTION STEPS

IF YOUR FRIEND HAS ASKED FOR YOUR HELP AND YOU ARE TOGETHER OR ON THE PHONE.

- Stay on the phone or in the same room until the attack is over.
- Pray out loud that God will send his angels to protect both of you and to encircle you.
- Out loud bind and cast out the demons harassing them in the name of Jesus Christ whose blood was shed on the cross for the forgiveness of your sins and theirs.
- Out loud thank God for the victory He has given us over Satan and encourage your friend that God has given them victory and they just have to claim it.
- Get your friend to say out loud that they bind and cast out the demons tormenting them in the name of Jesus Christ whose blood was shed on the cross for the forgiveness of their sins.
- Out loud thank God for his protection and for the angels that are keeping the demons out of the building.
- Stay on the phone or in the same room until peace begins to return and your friend is calmer and you can tell there is no active demonic attack happening.
- Check back in a few hours later or the next day to make sure they are okay.

IF YOU ARE HELPING WITHOUT BEING ASKED BUT YOU ARE WITH YOUR FRIEND OR ON THE PHONE

- Stay on the phone or in the same room until the attack is over.
- Pray silently that God will send his angels to protect both of you and to encircle you.
- Silently but forcefully bind and cast out the demons harassing them in the name of Jesus Christ whose blood was shed on the cross for the forgiveness of your sins and theirs.
- Silently thank God for the victory He has given us over Satan.
- Stay on the phone or in the same room until you can tell there is no active demonic attack happening.
- Check back in a few hours later or the next day to make sure they are okay.

IF YOU ARE HELPING YOUR FRIEND BUT CAN'T BE WITH THEM

- Picture your friend in your mind. If it helps you and you are able to, picture the space they are in as well. Imagine the demons as shadows around them.
- Ask God to send angels to protect you both.
- Bind and cast out the demons in the name of Jesus. Imagine the shadows being shoved out of the building by shafts of God's holy light.

- Thank God for the victory he has given us over Satan and ask for the continued protection of the angels for you and your friend.
- Check in on your friend frequently to see if you can sense any demons around them and repeat these steps as necessary.
- Talk to your friend when you are able to get a sense of how they are doing. If they know what you are doing teach them how to cast out demons themselves.

PRAYER OF VICTORY

Thank you God for giving me the strength to help others. Set your angels in a hedge around me and those who I am helping so that no demons can approach. Thank you for the victory you have given us over Satan and all the forces of darkness.

Help those that I care about learn to fight and stand on their own, claiming your victory as their own. Let me be the light that helps them and the shoulder that they can lean on. Guide my actions and my words that they might bring You glory and that I would only make things better never worse. I praise you my Protector and Deliverer for the might of Your hand. Amen.

Chapter 12
Sharing What You've Learned With Others

It used to be that it was nearly impossible for me to talk about my experiences with the supernatural, particularly the demonic, with other people. It was one thing to say that you could feel the presence of God's love or you felt that angels were ministering to you and quite another to say that you were being attacked by a demon. Most people don't like to talk about the things that frighten them. When I was growing up people didn't like to talk about Satan as a real entity and were not nearly as open about spiritual warfare as they are today. I was afraid of what other people would say and think if I started talking about it. For a girl who was experiencing torment almost daily this was a secret that was hard to keep and yet I felt I had to.

It used to be that if I felt like I was compelled to bring the subject up with someone, I would get so stressed out about it that I would literally go into shock. My temperature would drop, I'd feel faint, and I would begin to shake uncontrollably. This was induced through my own fear of talking about the topic and, I'm now convinced, through demonic interference to keep me from helping others who needed to hear what I had to say.

A shift happened a couple of years ago. God had been telling me for years that I needed to spread the word about what demons are and how we can vanquish them. I had been doing so on a very tiny scale. I knew He was calling me to tell the world and I was making strides in that direction, but I was still fearful. I slowly began to tell friends and family who didn't know about this area of my life about my experiences and that I planned to go public with them as my ministry.

God speaks to me through movies and television a lot. He knows that He can get to me that way even when I'm trying to ignore His messages. When the film *Hotel Transylvania* came out, I went to see it with my husband, expecting it to be a fun bit of fluff. (It is, by the way.) God, however, chose to use the film to hit me right between the eyes. The animated film depicts Dracula as an over-protective father who has created a hotel for monsters where they can come on vacation and be themselves and not worry about being attacked by angry mobs with pitchforks. It really is a very sweet father-daughter film and does a lovely job of portraying that relationship and the ways in which it changes as the daughter grows up. What struck me, though, was the sudden, unexpected jealousy I felt that these creatures could just go to this place and be themselves and not care what the world thought of them.

That was when God showed me just what hiding this part of my life had been costing me. By not allowing most of the people around me to know that the struggle with the supernatural was literally a part of my everyday life I was never able to fully relax around them and truly be myself. I was always guarding this part of me. He told me right there in that theater that the time had come to tell the world and that I couldn't care what the world thought. Two-and-a-half months later, I released a podcast where I let everyone who cared to listen know what I had known all my life. *Demons exist. They want to harm us. We need to fight back.*

I was afraid when I did that, but now I'm experiencing a wonderful sense of freedom and release. The secret I've kept bottled up for so many years is out and now I can finally start to use all my knowledge and experience to do some real good and to change more than one life at a time. I find that I'm even telling random strangers now what I once wouldn't tell my closest friends and I can do it with a joy deep in my soul and the knowledge that I'm finally being the person God made me to be. "The truth shall set you free" has become one of my favorite quotes when it comes to this area of life.

Despite my newfound boldness I can still occasionally have fits of nerves when talking to people. The one thing I know, though, is that you can't let that stop you. The demonic thrives in the dark, secret places where people are afraid to go. The more light and knowledge we shed on it the more it shrinks and flees. Plus, once you have a taste of freedom for yourself chances are you're going to want to help friends and family members as well.

CHOOSE AN APPROPRIATE TIME

When you decide to broach this topic with someone, choose a time where you can talk with them privately and you won't have pressing time constraints on you. Blurting it out in front of others or hastily trying to fit all the details into a five-minute conversation won't do anyone much good. Allow time for the other person to ask questions (they may or may not).

Be aware, though, that if it is important that you talk to this person, demons might try delaying tactics on you. If there simply is never a “right time”, then you’ll just have to choose a time that is good enough and start the conversation. Pray ahead of time that God will give you the time and privacy you need to say what you need to.

BE CALM

If you are agitated, the other person will likely become agitated as well. Pray for God’s peace to be on you while you speak. Take several deep cleansing breaths and banish any demons that may try to interfere with the conversation.

If there is something that you know relaxes you that would be appropriate for the occasion without being distracting, you might try utilizing that. For example, some of the most difficult conversations in my life have been made better by having them over bowls of ice cream.

If they get upset, force yourself to remain calm. No matter what they say or do you have to realize that they are reacting out of fear, doubt, anger, and quite possibly being manipulated by their own personal and family demons. Allowing them to push you out of your own calm certainty at this point will only harm both of you.

BE CLEAR

Know what you want to say and how you want to say it beforehand. Be matter-of-fact and don’t give off the appearance of being wishy-washy or doubting what you are saying. Make statements that are simple and direct. Don’t beat around the bush. Look at the other person to make sure they are understanding what you are saying. Don't be afraid to have them ask questions. Answer to the best of your ability and if you don't know something, don't be afraid to admit that either.

If you find yourself becoming uncertain or confused take a moment to re-center. Take a deep breath and banish any demons that are present. (You may do this silently as long as you put force and conviction behind it.) Ask God for clarity and resume the conversation.

BE PATIENT

Some people will grasp what you are saying more readily than others. Some will need a lot more explanation. Stay calm and be as patient as you can while you try to answer their questions. Remember, what you are saying might be a new concept to them or one that they are struggling to believe. People process information in different ways and at different speeds. Don't be surprised if you have to repeat yourself or if they ask the same questions days or weeks later. Help them understand what you are saying and make it as easy on them to talk to you as possible.

DON'T GET DISCOURAGED

Some people won't believe you. Their reactions may vary from silence and polite nodding to sarcasm and eye-rolling to downright hostility and argumentation. That's okay. They're not ready to accept the truth of what you're saying. There are a number of possible reasons for this. Some people might not believe in the existence of the supernatural at all. Some people weren't raised to believe in the existence of incarnate evil. Some people are too afraid to believe that it's real. Some people are too afraid of what it will mean for them if what you're saying is true.

Whatever their reason for doubt or disbelief, don't let it discourage you. Don't try to argue with them, but accept that this is not something they're willing to accept at this time. That doesn't mean that in a few months or years they won't be ready to talk to you on this subject. You've planted the seed, made your beliefs clear, and that's all you can do. In many ways it's similar to sharing any belief with somebody, including the gospel of Jesus. You just have to trust that when they're ready to talk, they will come to you. And they almost certainly will so long as you have been kind and open with them.

Just remember, the truth is on your side. No matter who denies it, that will not change. All you can do is pray for that person, fight on their behalf if the need arises, and trust that when and if they need to deal with the demonic that they will come to you or someone else for help.

BE PREPARED FOR DEMONIC INTERFERENCE

There's a reason why people say "Speak of the devil and he appears." Demons may try to interfere to keep you from getting your message across to the other person. They may also show up in a more overt fashion in an attempt to frighten one or both of you. I've had both of these things happen. Be on alert throughout the conversation and afterward for any signs of demonic interference and banish demons immediately upon detection.

KEY SCRIPTURES

"And ye shall know the truth, and the truth shall make you free." - John 8:32 (KJV)

ACTION STEPS

- Ask for God's guidance in choosing the right time and the right words.
- Choose a time when you will have some privacy and more than just a couple of minutes to talk.
- Pray for God's protection and peace during the conversation and afterward.
- Banish any demons present and bind your own personal or family demons from interfering. Banish any demons that show up throughout the conversation.
- Remain calm, focused, and patient.

PRAYER OF VICTORY

Thank you, God, for allowing me the opportunity to share what I'm going through with others and to help them with my knowledge and experiences. Thank you for letting them hear and understand me. I bind all demons that would interfere and cast them out in the name of Jesus Christ whose blood was shed on the cross for my sins. God, send angels to watch over us that we might not be disturbed and that our time together will be edifying for both of us. Thank You for being on the throne and granting us the ultimate victory over Satan today, tomorrow, and forever. Amen.

Chapter 13
Eternal Vigilance is the Price of Freedom

Sooner or later your time of intense demonic attack will pass. Take a deep breath and enjoy the calm. It may last a few days or even a few decades. However, that doesn't mean that you will never be attacked again. You almost certainly will be. Once things calm down you still need to remain alert and perform regular checkups on yourself in order to ensure that the enemy doesn't creep back into your life.

Eventually the spiritual warfare will ease up, either permanently or for a season. The more you put yourself out there, follow God's will, and live the life you were born to live the more Satan will want to stop you. But every victory you claim makes it that much harder for him to touch you. Strive for the day when God rewards you as Job and binds the devil from attacking you at every turn. In the meantime acknowledge demonic interference in your life as the enemy being afraid of you and what you are capable of and do everything in your power to thwart him at every turn.

GET IN THE HABIT OF PERFORMING REGULAR CHECK-UPS

It can seem like the battle against the demonic is a never-ending one. The good news is that we know that God defeats Satan and that is how the story ends. While the battle as a whole may not end until that time, there are seasons of rest and reprieve. Some people only experience periods of demonic interference a couple of times in their life while others will experience it much more frequently. As far as the Bible tells us, Job only had to deal with Satan during the one season of his life. Others have had to face him multiple times. Regardless of which path your life is going to take, it is important to remain vigilant. The enemy is always looking to see what kind of mischief he can cause in the life of believers.

To this end do an occasional check-up on your mental, physical, and spiritual state. Ask yourself if any hardships you're facing, dark thoughts that are filling you, or anything else is natural or unnatural. Most of the time injury or sickness are just afflictions that are common to being alive. Sometimes, however they are exploited, and in extreme cases, even caused by demonic forces.

The best thing to do is get into a habit of taking some quiet time to examine the various areas of your life for influence or interference. Banish anything dark that you find and ask God again for His protection. If doing this once a day seems daunting or time-consuming, consider doing it once a week. You can even make it a part of your Sunday worship routine to make it easier for you to remember to do weekly.

STAY ALERT TO THE WARNING SIGNS

Just because things are going well is no reason to let your guard down. You might go months or even years between spiritual attacks. Still, keep in mind the signs to look for regarding spiritual attack against yourself or others.

Remember that when demons find it difficult to win against you they can and often will try and come at you sideways through friends or loved ones. Make sure to do regular check-ups on those closest to you as well, especially during times of heightened stress or if you notice behavior that is out of character.

REMEMBER THAT PERIODS OF SPIRITUAL ATTACK OFTEN COINCIDE WITH PERIODS OF SPIRITUAL GROWTH

When Satan and his minions are hounding you, it's often a sign that you are on the right track. Times of intense spiritual growth are often accompanied by times of spiritual warfare. The enemy wants to keep you from reaching your God-given potential. It's the equivalent of someone waving their arms wildly in the air while jumping up and down and shouting in an attempt to distract you from seeing something they don't want you to see. Look at Job. Satan attacked him because he had found favor with God and Satan wanted to tear him down, distract him, turn him from the path.

I had a friend who was in a dysfunctional relationship that ended badly. Every time there was a moment of intense spiritual growth or breakthrough in my friend's life, the ex would call out of the blue and spend the next twenty-four hours filling up the voicemail with insane ramblings that would depress my friend and rip their attention away from God. That is, until my friend learned to recognize this as a spiritual attack meant to distract. Now, any time one of those calls comes in it is like they treat it like a seeing a big neon sign that says, "Congratulations, you're on the right path!"

I've learned a lot from my friend about viewing spiritual attacks as desperate attempts to keep me from doing something that will improve my life and my relationship with God. I can't quite laugh about them yet like my friend does, but I'm beginning to use them to sharpen my focus and press forward faster, knowing that I'm doing the right thing.

Learn to see these periods of attack in your life as signposts that you're heading in the right direction with your feet firmly on the path that God has set for you. In Mark chapter eight we read about how Jesus rebuked Peter saying "Get thee behind me, Satan." What had happened was that Jesus was talking openly with his disciples about the trials that were to befall him including his crucifixion and that he would then be resurrected. Peter, acting as an unwitting tool for the devil, tried to tell Jesus to stop talking about those things. The devil wanted to distract Jesus from his destiny and he was willing to use one of Jesus' closest friends to do it.

IF POSSIBLE, FIND AN ACCOUNTABILITY PARTNER TO CHECK IN WITH

I can't stress this one enough. When we are not actively confronted with the demonic on a regular basis our brains stop looking for signs of attack. We let thoughts or feelings we once would have suspected slip through the cracks without scrutiny. We slip back into old, destructive habits and complacency. Having someone who can force you to take a hard look at your own actions can help prevent backsliding into behaviors that open the way for the demonic to infest.

Make a habit of checking in with this person at least every other month if not more often. Set aside some time to connect either in person or on the phone and discuss your lives and spiritual progress reports. Challenge each other's assumptions and encourage each other to stretch in your spiritual walk.

I have a small group of people whom I can rely on to tell me when something I say or do seems off in some way or if they think some trial I'm going through smacks of demonic interference in my life. Through the years we've gotten to know and trust each other and when one person in that group says "demon" everyone else says "fight". We each do spiritual check-ups on each other without being asked and report immediately if we find something one or all of us needs to be aware of.

This position of accountability partner requires absolute trust and absolute honesty. You have to allow the person to give you the truth even if you don't want to hear it. When they do remember that it's with your blessing and for your benefit. So, no shooting the messenger! There are times when one of my accountability partners has given me a truth I didn't want to deal with and I've let them know that I hated them in that moment. They've said the same to me. We're not allowed to hold a grudge, though, because what we are doing we are doing out of love for one another and a desire to see each other be everything God wants us to be.

KEY SCRIPTURES

"And when the devil had ended all the temptation, he departed from him for a season."

- Luke 4:13 (KJV)

"Be sober, be vigilant; because your adversary the devil walks about like a roaring lion, seeking whom he may devour."

- I Peter 5:8 (NKJV)

ACTION STEPS

- Once a week check in with yourself and examine the various areas of your life for tell-tale signs of demonic interaction.
- If any signs of demonic influence or interference are detected, act accordingly.
- Be aware of signs of demonic influence regarding those around you.
- Find an accountability partner and check in with them at least every other month if not more often.

PRAYER OF VICTORY

Thank you, dear God, for the victory you have given me over Satan and all his minions. Help me to relax in safety and peace and keep me from the snares of the enemy. Allow me rest but help me to be alert to the least signs of demonic interference in my life and the lives of those close to me. Help me to respond swiftly when need be and help me to grow closer to You. Thank you that my feet are on the path that You have set before me, and let nothing turn me from it. Allow me to be a blessing to others and shine light on the darkness that would encroach on their lives. Surround me with those who will watch out for me as I watch out for them. Keep us all in Your care now and forevermore. Amen.

Recommended Reading

Scripture

Genesis 3:1-24 - Temptation by Satan and the Fall of Man
Job - Torment and Temptation of Job by Satan
Matthew 4:1-11 - Temptation of Jesus by Satan

Non-Fiction Books

Battlefield of the Mind by Joyce Meyer
I Declare: 31 Promises to Speak Over Your Life by Joel Osteen
Open Mind, Open Heart by Thomas Keating

Novels

This Present Darkness by Frank Peretti
Piercing the Darkness by Frank Peretti

Look for

Battlefield Victory Workbook

Coming Winter 2014

Debbie Viguié is the New York Times Bestselling author of thirty novels including the *Wicked* series, the *Crusade* series and the *Wolf Springs Chronicles* series co-authored with Nancy Holder. Debbie also writes thrillers including *The Psalm 23 Mysteries,* the *Kiss* trilogy, and the *Witch Hunt* trilogy. While Debbie is primarily known for her fiction, she has spent years studying aspects of the demonic across all major religions. She has a passion for helping others to find freedom from demonic oppression. Her first book on the topic will be out in 2013 with more following in 2014. When Debbie isn't busy writing she enjoys spending time with her husband, Scott, visiting theme parks.

www.ingramcontent.com/pod-product-compliance
Lightning Source LLC
Chambersburg PA
CBHW061731020426
42331CB00006B/1202

9780615938592